## The HomeBuilders
### COUPLES SERIES
"Unless the Lord builds the house,
they labor in vain who build it."
Psalm 127:1

# RESOLVING CONFLICT IN MARRIAGE
## Leader's Guide

Bob and Jan Horner

# How to Let
# The Lord Build Your House
*and not labor in vain*

The Family Ministry is a part of Campus Crusade for Christ International, an evangelical Christian organization founded in 1951 by Bill Bright. The Family Ministry was started in 1976 to help fulfill the Great Commission by strengthening marriages and families and then equipping them to go to the world with the Gospel of Jesus Christ. Our Family Life Conference is held in most major cities throughout the United States and is one of the fastest-growing marriage conferences in America today. Information on all resources offered by the Family Ministry may be obtained by either writing or calling us at the address and telephone number listed below.

**The HomeBuilders Couples Series:** A small-group Bible study dedicated to making your family all that God intended.

**Resolving Conflict in Marriage—Leader's Guide**
ISBN 0–8499–8341–X

Unless otherwise indicated, Scripture quotations used are from the New American Standard Bible, copyright 1960, 1962, 1968, 1971 by The Lockman Foundation, used by permission. Scripture quotations marked NIV are from the New International Version of the Bible, copyright 1978 by the New York International Bible Society. Used by permission of Zondervan Bible Publishers.

Dennis Rainey, Director
**Family Ministry**
P.O. Box 23840
Little Rock, AR 72221-3840
(501) 223-8663

**A Ministry of Campus Crusade for Christ International**
Bill Bright, Founder and President

# CONTENTS

# ACKNOWLEDGMENTS

There is a Book which gives hope. It is "profitable for teaching, for reproof, for correction, for training in righteousness; that the man [and woman] of God may be adequate, equipped for every good work" (2 Timothy 3:16–17). Certainly marriage is a "good work." We are grateful to the One who inspired the Bible, and to His Son, for providing the basis for resolving all conflict.

Campus Crusade for Christ has provided the nurturing environment needed for our twenty-three-year marriage. We have been given vision for our lives, time to grow up, training, and the privilege of working among the finest associates possible. You have helped us to know and love the Author of marriage.

The Merediths, founders of the Family Ministry, were the first to give us workable solutions to conflicts we discovered in our marriage. Don and Sally, thank you for the friendship!

Dennis and Barb Rainey are not only the visionaries behind The HomeBuilders Couples Series and thus this study, but are favorite friends and co-workers who have "pushed" us into speaking and writing with the Family Ministry. Thanks for the loving shove, you two!

Ideas and concepts need the shaping of craftsmen. Julie Denker and Dave Boehi, you have chiseled and sanded and polished our work into something to which we are proud to give our signature. We have told you more than once, and we say it again, "You are geniuses!"

To the many groups around the country who first piloted this project . . . thanks for the feedback. Your input was invaluable. You will likely see those contributions as you use this study again.

There really is nothing new under the sun. This study has evolved out of learning from favorite authors such as Paul Tournier, James Dobson, Gary Smalley, H. Norman Wright, Ed Wheat, and Willard F. Harley, Jr., and from some of our favorite people who work alongside us as fellow speakers with the Family Ministry.

# FOREWORD

Conflict is a common denominator of every marriage. No relationship is free from the friction caused by our differences and expectations—and just by being human. Repeatedly this subject is mentioned by our Family Life Conference guests as one of the most critical issues they face in their marriages. Yet few have received the training they need to know how to handle the hurt, misunderstandings, and difficulties encountered in a normal marriage relationship successfully.

That's why I asked Bob and Jan Horner to tackle this thorny problem—to equip you with practical "how-to's" for resolving conflict between husband and wife. For the past twenty-five years, as staff members with the Campus Crusade for Christ, the Horners have teamed up to enrich the lives of college students and lay couples all around the world. Since 1982, they have spoken to thousands annually as speakers at our Family Life Conference. And, for the last two years, they've written and fieldtested this material with couples just like you.

You'll find that Bob and Jan have blended together strong biblical principles with practical questions and projects that will challenge you to change the way you think about conflict. The Horners are in touch with the needs of couples and individuals today, and I am confident that their study will encourage you to dig to new and deeper levels of communication as husband and wife.

DENNIS RAINEY
Director of Family Ministry

# The HomeBuilders

## C O U P L E S   S E R I E S

"Unless the Lord builds the house,
they labor in vain who build it."
Psalm 127:1

# INTRODUCTION

Do you remember the first time you fell in love? That junior high—or elementary school—crush stirred your affections with little or no effort on your part. We use the term "falling in love" to describe the phenomenon of suddenly discovering our emotions have been captured by someone delightful.

Unfortunately, our society tends to make us think that all loving relationships should be equally as effortless. Thus, millions of couples, Christians included, approach their marriages certain that their "love for each other" will carry them through any difficulties. And millions of couples quickly learn that a good marriage does not happen automatically.

Otherwise intelligent people, who would not think of buying a car, investing money, or even going to the grocery store without some initial planning, enter into marriage with no plan of how to make their marriage succeed.

But God has already provided the plan, a set of blueprints for a truly godly marriage. His plan is designed to enable two people to grow together in a mutually satisfying relationship, and then to look beyond their own marriage to others. Ignoring this plan leads to isolation and separation between husband and wife, the pattern so evident in the majority of homes today. Even when great energy is expended, failure to follow God's blueprints results in wasted effort, bitter disappointment—and, in far too many cases, divorce.

In response to this need in marriages today, the Family Ministry of Campus Crusade for Christ is developing a series of small-group Bible studies called The HomeBuilders Couples Series. This series is designed to answer one question for couples:

### How do you build a distinctively Christian marriage?

It is our hope that in answering this question with the biblical blueprints for building a home, we will see the development of growing, thriving marriages filled with the love of Jesus Christ.

The Family Ministry of Campus Crusade for Christ is committed to strengthening your family. We hope The HomeBuilders Couples Series will assist you and your church as it equips couples in building godly homes.

This study, *Resolving Conflict in Marriage,* exists for those who wish to have their conflicts produce greater communication and understanding in their homes. It is composed of six sessions, each built around a concept which will enrich marriages. As you lead the sessions, you will help each individual and couple discover vital principles, personally interact with others, and then apply what they learn to their own marriages.

### How is the Bible used in this study?

You will notice as you proceed through this study that the Bible is referred to frequently as the final authority on the issues of life and marriage. Although written centuries ago, this Book still speaks clearly and powerfully about conflicts and struggles men and women face. The Bible is God's Word and contains His blueprints for building a godly home and for dealing with the practical issues of living.

While Scripture has only one primary interpretation, there may be several appropriate applications. Some of the passages used in this series were not originally written with marriage in mind, but they can be applied practically to the husband-wife relationship.

Encourage each group member to have a Bible along for each session. The New American Standard Version, the New International Version and the New King James Version are three excellent English translations which make the Bible easy to understand.

### What are the ground rules for these sessions?

These sessions are designed to be enjoyable and informative—and nonthreatening. Three simple ground rules will help ensure that everyone feels comfortable and gets the most out of the study.

1. Share nothing about your marriage which will embarrass your mate.

2. You may "pass" on any question you do not want to answer.

3. Each time between sessions, complete the **HomeBuilders Project** (questions for each couple to discuss and act on). Share one result at the next group meeting.

**What is this study intended to accomplish?**

Couples who participate in these sessions will find the experience:

▸ stimulates them to examine what Scripture says about how to construct a solid, satisfying marriage;

▸ allows them to interact with each other on a regular basis about significant issues in their marriages;

▸ encourages them to interact with other couples, establishing mutual accountability for growth efforts;

▸ motivates them to take specific actions which have been valuable to couples desiring to build stronger homes; and

▸ creates accountability to others for growth in their marriages.

**How many couples should be in this group?**

Four to seven couples, including you and your mate, is the optimum group size. Fewer than four may put too much pressure on some individuals, stifling their freedom to grow. More than seven will not allow solid relationships to develop among all the couples involved.

OTHER OPTIONS: With capable leadership, this study may be used effectively in other settings, such as:

▸ a counselor meeting weekly with one couple;

▸ two couples who know each other well and share the responsibility for the sessions;

▸ one couple who wishes to go through the study privately (I would encourage you, however, to make your ultimate goal that of taking

9

others through this study or participating in a small group; account-ability is essential for godly marriages); or

▶ a Sunday school leader who can creatively adapt it to a larger group setting. Some people will feel more comfortable in a larger group, but their sense of commitment to complete the **Construction** sections and **HomeBuilders Projects** may be reduced.

## What does it take to lead this study?

▶ First, you and your mate need to commit to each other and to God that this study will be a major priority for both of you.

▶ Second, you will need to work together to enlist other couples to participate in the group.

▶ Third, one of you will need to give time (at least one or two hours) each week to prepare for the session while the other takes the initiative to stay in touch with group members and to handle all the details of hospitality.

▶ And fourth, it is recommended that you pray regularly for each couple in your group.

## What is the session leader's job?

Try on the title of "facilitator"—a directive guide who encourages people to think, to discover what Scripture says, and to interact with others in the group. You are not being asked to be a lecturer, but neither are you to let group members ramble aimlessly and pool their ignorance. The directions in this handbook will help you keep each session moving.

## Do you have any tips for actually leading the group?

Here are four:

1. Keep the focus on what Scripture says, not on you or your ideas—or those of the group members, either. When someone disagrees with Scripture, affirm him or her for wrestling with the issue and point out

that some biblical statements are hard to understand or to accept. Encourage the person to keep an open mind on the issue at least through the remainder of the study.

2. Strive for balanced participation.

▶ A good way to encourage a nonparticipator to respond is to ask him or her to share an opinion or a personal experience rather than posing a question that can be answered "yes" or "no" or that requires a specific correct answer.

▶ The overly talkative person can be kept in control by the use of devices that call for responses in a specific manner (and which also help group members get to know little things about each other):

— "I'd like this question to be answered first by the husband of the couple with the next anniversary."

— ". . . the wife of the couple who had the shortest engagement."

— ". . . any husband who knows his mother-in-law's maiden name."

— ". . . anyone who complained about doing the last session's project."

▶ Other devices for guiding responses from the group include:

— Go around the group in sequence with each person commenting about a particular question without repeating what anyone else has said.

— Ask couples to talk with each other about a question, then have whichever partner has said the least so far in this session report on his or her answer.

— Limit answers to one or two sentences—or to 30 seconds each.

3. Encourage a person who gives a wrong or incomplete answer to look again at the question or the Scripture being explored. Offer a comment

such as, "That's really close," or "There's something else we need to see there." Or ask others in the group to respond. Avoid labeling an answer as "wrong"; doing so can kill the atmosphere for discussion.

4. Protect the application (**Construction**) times at the middle and end of the session. Be aware of the common tendency to avoid taking action by getting embroiled in a discussion. Even if some issues are not fully resolved, encourage people to place the topic on hold and move on to planning specific actions to take. Personal application is at the heart of this study.

### What is the best setting for group meetings?

Your living room is probably the best place to use. Inviting couples to your home is usually easier and friendlier than trying to get them to come to a room at church. You need a room where everyone can sit comfortably and see and hear each other.

Avoid letting couples or persons sit outside the group; they will not feel included. The seating arrangement is very important to discussion and involvement. If your home will not work, see if another couple in the group is willing to host the sessions.

### What about using the study in a Sunday school class?

While the study is designed primarily for small groups meeting in a home, a classroom can be used effectively if chairs are set up with round tables or just in circles of six or eight. For variety in some sessions, you may want to set the chairs in a large semicircle (with more than one row if necessary). Avoid straight rows that leave people seeing only the backs of heads.

### What about refreshments?

If you want a comfortable, relaxed setting that encourages people to get to know one another, something to sip and swallow is almost essential. But food should not become the focus of the session. Depending on the time of your meeting, you may find it works well to serve a beverage and light "munchies" as people arrive, then offer a dessert at the close of the study to encourage people to continue talking with each other for a while.

## What time schedule should we plan to follow?

A two-hour block is best. The time for the actual study is 60–90 minutes. The longer time period allows you to move at a more relaxed pace through each part of the session.

Once the people in your group get to know each other and interaction gets underway, you may find it difficult to complete a session in the time allotted. It is not necessary that every question be covered, and many are intended to stimulate thought, not to result in exhaustive discussion and resolution of the issue. Be sensitive to your use of time and be careful not to make comments about time pressure which will make the group feel rushed. For example:

▶ When you need to move the discussion to the next item, say something like, "We could probably talk about that question the rest of the evening, but we need to consider several other important questions that bear on this issue."

▶ When it's necessary to reduce or eliminate the time spent on a later question, simply say, "You can see that there are several more questions we could have moved on to discuss, but I felt we were making real progress, so I chose to spend some extra time on the earlier points."

You will find, as you prepare and review for each session, that some questions or sections are more relevant to your group than other portions of the study. Pace your study in such a way that those questions which must be addressed are not rushed.

*You are the leader* of your group and know the needs of the individual couples best. But keep in mind that the Holy Spirit will have an agenda for couples which you may never know about. "The mind of man plans his way, but the Lord directs his steps" (Proverbs 16:9). Do your best to prepare and pray over the session and then leave the results to God.

Plan an additional 30 minutes for fellowship, 5 or 10 minutes of which may precede the study and the remainder follow it. When you invite people, tell them to plan on the total time. This avoids having people rush off and not get acquainted. During the school year, 7:30–9:30 allows people to get home from work and get babysitters if needed.

Also, when you invite people to attend, let them know that the study will go for six sessions. People like to know how long they are committing themselves.

### How can we fit this into a Sunday school hour?

Clearly, something will have to squeeze. If you follow the shorter time guideline for each segment of the sessions, all the content and projects can fit in a 60-minute session. That leaves no room for traditional activities such as singing, announcements, etc. You will need to make a strong point that the full 60 minutes will be used to the hilt in each session.

People who are used to slipping in late may need an extra nudge to get there on time. The informal fellowship dimension which is vital to helping people feel at home in the group can be done to a degree before and after the session. The leader will need to be very sensitive to using the time wisely, since people may have other commitments that keep them from lingering.

You also might consider dividing each session into two parts and using two weeks of Sunday school for each one.

### Whom should we invite to participate?

The concepts in this study will benefit any couple, whether long-married, newlywed, engaged, or even just looking ahead to the possibilities of marriage. Leading the group will be easier if your group is made up of couples at similar stages in their relationships. The more they have in common, the easier it will be for them to identify with one another and open up in sharing.

On the other hand, it can also be helpful for a couple to gain a fresh viewpoint on marriage by interacting with a couple having significantly different experiences. In other words, if a couple is interested in building and maintaining a strong marriage, they belong in this study.

### What if one partner doesn't want to participate?

Expect some people, especially some husbands, to attend the first session wishing they were someplace else. Some will be there just because their mate or another couple nagged them to come. Some may be suspicious of a "Bible" study. Others may be fearful of revealing any weaknesses in their marriage. And some may feel either that their marriage is beyond help or that they do not need any help.

You can dispel a great deal of anxiety and resistance at the first session. Simply begin by mentioning that you know there are probably some who came reluctantly. Share a few reasons people may feel that way, and affirm that regardless of why anyone has come, you are pleased each person is there.

Briefly comment on how the concepts in this study have helped you and your marriage and express your confidence that each person will enjoy the study and benefit from it. Also, assure the group that at no time will anyone be forced to share publicly. What each person shares is his or her choice—no one will be embarrassed.

### Does each session follow a format?

Yes. The following outline gives a quick look at how the sessions are structured:

▶ **FOCUS**—a statement of the overall focus of the session you will be studying.

▶ **WARM UP**—a time to help people get to know each other, review the past session, and begin the new study.

▶ **BLUEPRINTS**—the biblical content of the session.

▶ **CONSTRUCTION**—the application of the session—a small project done privately as a couple during the session.

▶ **HOMEBUILDERS PRINCIPLES**—summary points made throughout the study.

▶ **MAKE A DATE**—a time for couples to decide when they will complete their **HomeBuilders Project.**

▶ **HOMEBUILDERS PROJECT**—a 60–90 minute project to be completed at home before the next session.

▶ **RECOMMENDED READING**—suggestions for use of several books to get maximum value from the study.

Although the format shown may vary slightly from session to session, you should familiarize yourself with it so that you are aware of the purpose of each segment of the study. Explaining the segments to your group will also aid them in understanding the session's content.

### Can a non-Christian participate in this study?

The study is definitely targeted at Christians, but you may find a non-Christian couple or individual who wants to build a strong marriage and is willing to participate. Welcome the non-Christian into your group and seek to get to know the person or couple during the early weeks of the study.

Before you get to Session Five, schedule a time to meet with this person or couple privately to explain the principles on which this study is built. Share Christ and offer an opportunity by faith to receive Him as Savior and Lord. We recommend "The Four Spiritual Laws" to help you explain how a person can know God. They are included as an appendix to the study guide and the leader's guide.

### How does this study fit into the total strategy for building Christian marriages?

While this six-session study has great value in itself, it is only the first step in a long-term process of growth. If people complete these sessions and then gradually return to their previous patterns of living, little or no good will result. Continued effort is required for people to initiate and maintain new directions in their marriages.

It is our belief, also, that no couple can truly build a Christian home and marriage without a strong commitment and involvement in a local church.

The church provides the daily spiritual direction and equipping necessary for a truly godly marriage.

The Family Ministry of Campus Crusade is committed to changing the destiny of the family and providing quality resources to build distinctively Christian marriages. The HomeBuilders Couples Series is designed to help couples understand and obtain essential components important to building committed Christian marriages and Christian families. Several books are now available, and many more are planned for future availability. Those available now are:

▶ *Building Your Marriage*—the basic introduction of God's principles for marriage.

▶ *Strengthening Your Mate's Self-Esteem*—a unique plan of building blocks to strengthen your mate's self-image.

▶ *Building Teamwork in Marriage*—designed for men and women to explore God's purpose for their lives, their roles, responsibilities, and differentness.

▶ *Mastering Your Money in Marriage*—developed to help couples identify and grapple with the whole concept of a biblical approach to finances and to provide practical guidance in planning personal finances.

## What should I expect group members to do at the end of these sessions?

As you prepare this study, prayerfully consider each couple in your group and the most appropriate next step to recommend they take when the study is completed:

1. Encourage them to commit to participate in another study, such as *Building Your Marriage*. Decide whether you or someone else will lead the study and when you would schedule it. Since some people in your group may not continue to the next study, it may be wise to schedule the other study after several more groups have completed this one. However, if you wait too long, you and your group members may lose the momentum built through this study.

2. Some couples in your group may be candidates to lead their own group in studying *Resolving Conflict in Marriage*. Raise the possibility, even though their first reaction may be "We don't know enough to be leaders!" Assure them that sharing what they have learned with others is the best way to continue learning. And obviously, if *you* can lead this study, *they* certainly can as well. Remember, the more couples who go through this book, the more couples you will have ready for another one.

Expect many to continue through The HomeBuilders Couples Series. Relationships established in the earlier studies will cause most group members to want to continue.

### What about resources that would be particularly helpful in leading this study?

1. If you have attended our Family Life Conference, then your conference manual should be a great resource. If you have not attended, it may be appropriate for your group to come to the conference when it comes to your area.

2. Other resources are suggested at the end of each session.

### Are there any tips for leading this study?

1. Encourage couples to do the **HomeBuilders Project** between each session. This is where they will *really* learn. Do your best to hold them accountable without offending them. People need the accountability this study affords.

2. Do not let the sessions drag, become dull and boring, or go too long. Be sensitive to the needs of the group and watch their attention span—when people stop contributing, they may have stopped listening as well. It is far better for people to wish the session could have gone longer than for them to wish it had ended sooner. Keep it moving. Keep it lively. Keep it going!

3. Don't be afraid of a question that is greeted with group silence—some of the best answers come after moments of silent thought. Keep in mind as a group leader that 15 seconds can seem like 5 minutes.

4. Again, these sessions contain plenty of material to keep you going. You need not fear that you will run out of stimulating material. Be directive. Lead the group.

One further tip: If you find one or two particularly profound questions that you really want everyone to consider, why not have group members pause to consider the question individually and then write and share their answers with the group? Moments of silence and self-evaluation can be among the sharpest tools for truly teaching others. Use silence and these moments of evaluation strategically and sparingly.

**One last question: What is the purpose of this leader's guide?**

This book and the suggestions that are made are meant to cause your creative juices to flow, not to cramp your style. You will undoubtedly come up with some creative ways to instruct and teach this material. That's fine. Don't let these recommendations force you into a box.

If, however, you find it difficult to be creative as a facilitator, this guide will relieve your fears. In it you will find ideas, questions, and tips that will help you keep the study moving.

Those of you who have used the HomeBuilders Couples Series before will find a different format with this leader's guide. The entire text of the study guide (including **Construction** and **HomeBuilders Projects**) is reprinted here, along with the tips for the leader and answers to the study guide questions. All answers, tips, and notes appear in italics to distinguish them from the study guide material. And the page number for each study guide question is added in parentheses for easy reference.

As a couple, use this guide to prepare for the session, regardless of the type of person you are. One good question on a hot topic can spawn great discussion and interaction. Remember, this study is for these couples' marriages and their application.

## HOMEBUILDERS PRINCIPLES

**HomeBuilders Principle #1:** Understanding differences between you and your mate is the first step toward resolving conflict.

**HomeBuilders Principle #2:** Unresolved conflict creates a potent acid which eats away at a marriage and family.

**HomeBuilders Principle #3:** A peaceful relationship with your mate is possible when you pursue God's peace in your life.

**HomeBuilders Principle #4:** Love, commitment, and forgiveness provide the environment for a person to be willing to be known by another.

**HomeBuilders Principle #5:** To enjoy the privileges of transparency, you need to control the power of the tongue.

**HomeBuilders Principle #6:** A commitment to becoming a better listener will help you avoid many conflicts and resolve others before they grow too difficult.

**HomeBuilders Principle #7:** For confrontation to benefit a relationship, truth must be shared with love.

**HomeBuilders Principle #8:** You must forgive your mate as God has forgiven you.

**HomeBuilder's Principle #9:** The power of forgiveness lies in God's Spirit as He is given control in your heart.

**HomeBuilders Principle #10:** Forgiving your mate sets you free to experience love and oneness.

**HomeBuilders Principle #11:** Returning a blessing for an insult helps defeat the cycle of selfishness which can corrode a marriage relationship.

**HomeBuilders Principle #12:** As you depend on the Holy Spirit for wisdom and power, you will develop the forgiving and gracious heart you need to respond with a blessing rather than an insult.

## A WORD ABOUT RESOLVING CONFLICT

Conflict is inevitable. The difference between any two couples is not *whether* there is conflict, but *what* the partners do with it when it surfaces. *Resolving Conflict in Marriage* has been prepared for those who wish to have their conflicts produce greater communication and understanding with their mates.

As a couple, you will not be required (or even invited) to relate your personal conflicts within the group. However, you will be encouraged to uncover, discuss, and resolve those conflicts alone as a couple. This study surfaces issues that many couples have carefully suppressed or have purposely ignored. Defusing these "time bombs" is difficult but oh, so necessary; therefore, don't be surprised if it seems you are experiencing *greater* conflict during this study than before you began. It is all part of learning the joy that comes with communication and understanding.

We commend you for investing in your marriage by rolling up your sleeves and digging into what is so important to you and the generations that will follow you—*Resolving Conflict in Marriage.*

BOB AND JAN HORNER

## SESSION ONE
*Recognizing Conflict*

### FOCUS

God's design for marriage
leads to a peaceful relationship
between husband and wife.
Conflict can build this
relationship through communication
and understanding.

### Objectives

You will help your group members sharpen their awareness of how they deal with conflict as you guide them to:

■ Examine factors which contribute to conflict in a relationship;

■ Discuss current sources of conflict; and

■ Discover scriptural guidance about settling differences.

### Overall Comments

1. Session One sets the tone for the study by establishing friendly, honest interaction in the group about the topic of conflict. Some couples may claim they "never argue," while others may engage in one battle royal after another. In any case, this session will help each one recognize that the differences that exist between people are inevitable sources of friction in any relationship. Rather than presenting all conflict as a negative,

this session will help couples discern the ways in which differences help to foster understanding and growth in each individual and in the marriage relationship.

2. Be sure you have a study guide for each individual. You will also want to have a Bible and extra pens or pencils for group members who may have forgotten to bring one.

OPTION: Personally distribute the study guides several days before this first session. Ask group members to read the introductory material in the study guide to lay the groundwork for the study.

### Starting the First Session

Start the session on time, even if everyone is not yet present. Briefly share a few positive feelings about leading this study:

■ Express your interest in strengthening your own marriage and dealing positively with conflict.

■ Admit that your marriage and the way you manage conflict in marriage are not perfect.

■ State that the concepts in this study have been helpful in your marriage.

■ Recognize that various individuals or couples may have been reluctant to come (pressured by spouse or friend, wary of a "Christian" group, sensitive about problems with marriage and/or conflict, stress in schedule that makes it difficult to set aside the time for this series, etc.).

■ Thank group members for their interest and willingness to participate.

Hand out the study guides if you have not already done so, and give a quick overview of The HomeBuilders Couples Series and this study guide. Briskly leaf through the study guide and point out three or four topics and the benefits of studying them. Don't be afraid to do a little selling here—people need to know how they personally are going to profit from the study. They also need to know where this series will take them, especially if they are even a little bit apprehensive about the group.

Explain the format for each session in no more than 2 or 3 minutes, using Session One as your example. Each session contains the following components:

▶ **FOCUS**—a capsule statement of the main point of the session.

▶ **WARM UP**—a time to get better acquainted with each other and to begin thinking of the session topic.

▶ **BLUEPRINTS**—discovering God's purposes and plans for marriage.

▶ **HOMEBUILDERS PRINCIPLES**—summary points made throughout the study.

▶ **CONSTRUCTION**—applying something that was learned, usually working as a couple.

▶ **MAKE A DATE**—a time to decide *when* during the week they will complete the **HomeBuilders Project.**

▶ **HOMEBUILDERS PROJECT**—an hour during the week when husband and wife interact with the implications of what was learned. *These times are really the heart of the series.*

▶ **RECOMMENDED READING**—books that couples can read together to get maximum benefit from the study.

Call attention to the "ground rules" for the sessions which are printed on page 11 of the study guide and pages 8–9 of this leader's guide.

*Note:* In the sections to come, material that appears in the study guide is presented in regular type and added material for the leader appears in italics.

## WARM UP
(25–40 minutes)

> *The **Warm Up** is intended to set a friendly, enjoyable tone from the opening minutes. Even if your group is already well-acquainted, these **Warm Up** activities have great value in helping everyone relax and make the transition from the day's pressures.*

1. *Begin by asking each couple to be ready to answer the introductory questions about themselves:* Introduce yourself to the group by relating the following information *(p. 18)*:

   ▶ Name, occupation, town where you grew up;

   ▶ Months/years you dated as a couple;

   ▶ How and where you met.

   _____

   _____

   _____

   _____

   *Tip: Ask your mate to share this information about your relationship as a couple. As people share, have everyone write down in their study guide at least one interesting fact about each couple.*

2. What kinds of conflict do you remember having during your first year of marriage? *(p. 18)*

   _____

   _____

3. *Note: This last question is optional. It's a different type of question, and you may not want to use it if you feel the group wouldn't respond to it:*

   Which of the following animals (or blend of animals) best characterize the way you communicate at home? If you can't find a match, make up your own. (Circle your choice/s.) *(p. 19)*

   ▶ Beagle (friendly and outgoing)

   ▶ Porcupine (a little difficult to get close to)

   ▶ Turtle Dove (cheery in the mornings)

   ▶ Owl (good at evening conversations)

▶ African Lion (a lot of "roar" around the house)

▶ Clam (hard to open up)

▶ Kitten (just give me your lap and I'll purr indefinitely)

Which one would you use to describe your mate? *(p. 19)*

---

*Tip: Suggest that it might be fun to identify with an animal or a bird. It would be good if both you and your spouse begin this one, suggesting that in no way should you use an animal that puts down your mate.*

## BLUEPRINTS
(20–30 minutes)

*This Blueprints section seeks to raise awareness of the inevitability of conflict in a relationship and some of the common causes of such conflict.*

## A. Conflict Is Inevitable

Marriage is an attempt to blend together two distinctly different individuals with differing backgrounds, values, personalities, and male/female distinctives. Conflicts under these conditions are inevitable.

*Have someone in the group read the following case study aloud:*

### CASE STUDY

They met at the concessions stand at the Frontier Days Rodeo one cool Wyoming evening. They laughed when each of them ordered exactly the same thing—burger without mustard and onions, cherry soft drink, and large fries. They already had at least that much in common.

In fact, they discovered they both loved horses, the mountains, and being away from home. Wyoming seemed to be the right place to connect two people from such opposite parts of the United States. Carrie, now a stockbroker, was raised around horses. Her earliest memories were populated with world-class jumpers. Her bedroom bulletin board was covered with blue ribbons.

Carrie's parents sent her off to college from their home in one of Southern California's most luxurious country-club estates. She originally came to the University of Wyoming to major in business and minor in equestrian science, and after graduation she remained in Wyoming because she loved the area.

When Rick heard the term "country club," he figured it was probably something you carry for self defense when traveling overseas. The small Tennessee mountain farm where he grew up provided only the very basics for life. But from an early age, Rick knew a lot about horses; his dad always managed to have a few around.

Rick had moved to Wyoming five years earlier so he could work on a ranch and see the greatest rodeos in the world. Then he met Carrie, and the idea of staying out West started to look pretty good.

1. As a casual observer, can you see any differences that you think will need attention if Rick and Carrie begin a serious relationship? What are they? *(p. 21)*

   ***Possible Answers:*** *Cultural, financial, background, professional, educational.*

2. What sorts of conflict can you foresee emerging from these differences? *(p. 21)*

   ***Possible Answers:*** *In-laws, financial perspective, long-term compatibility.*

*Tip: Be prepared to suggest some answers and ask group members to tell how they imagine Rick and Carrie might clash in each area.*

3. Why is it essential for a married couple to learn how to resolve conflict in their relationship? *(p. 21)*

**Answer:** *Conflict is inevitable for every couple; if you don't learn how to resolve it, your relationship will deteriorate.*

4. Many other factors can produce conflict in marriage. One is *personality differences* (gregarious vs. solitary, easygoing vs. perfectionistic, emotional vs. reserved, etc.). How can this cause strife? *(p. 21)*

**Answer:** *People often choose a mate with a different personality; at first this is an attraction, but at a later date it can also be an irritant. There's a tendency to wish that your mate would act like you do, and when this doesn't occur, the result is strife.*

5. What types of *differing values and philosophies* (about finances, religion, raising children, etc.) produce conflict in marriage? What types of conflicts over these differences have you observed—either in your marriage or in someone else's relationship? *(p. 22)*

**Possible Answers:** *Regarding finances, one partner may be a free spender while the other likes to keep to a strict budget. Regarding religion, there will be obvious conflict if one person has a strong faith in God while the other does not. Differing views about styles of worship, points of doctrine, types of ministry, etc., can cause strife. Regarding children, couples might argue about how to discipline, what schools to choose, what clothes to buy (and how much to spend on clothes), what extracurricular activities the children should be involved in, and more. Conflict also can arise over differing philosophies on issues such as punctuality, keeping promises, division of household duties, amount of time spent watching television, and many other subjects.*

6. How do *differences between men and women* bring about conflict?"*(p. 22)*

**Answer:** *Men and women often think and act differently, and often they aren't sensitive enough to try to see things from the other person's perspective.*

7. What is it that women typically don't understand about men? *(p. 22)*

*Possible Answers: (There are many answers to this question; these are just a few.) Women often fail to realize how important work is to many men. They often don't understand that many men are motivated by challenge. (When they were dating, she was the challenge. Now he may be challenged by other things, like work, sports, etc.) Men often have a stronger sex drive, especially in the early years of marriage, and they are sexually motivated by what they see more than women are.*

*Tip: Call on the men to suggest some typical misunderstandings women make about men.*

8. What is it that men typically don't understand about women? *(p. 22)*

*Possible Answers: (Again, these are just a few of the possible answers.) Men sometimes fail to realize how much importance their wives place on the emotional side of a relationship. Women are often more need-oriented than men. They are often more intuitive in their thinking. They're often more sensitive than men in expressing feelings.*

*Tip: Allow the women a chance to mention some typical male misunderstandings about women.*

*Read aloud* **HomeBuilders Principle #1: Understanding differences between you and your mate is the first step toward resolving conflict.**

**B. The Impact of Conflict**

1. Ephesians 4:26 reads, "Be angry, and yet do not sin; do not let the sun go down on your anger."

   a. What does "do not let the sun go down on your anger" mean? *(p. 22)*

   *Answer: Do not go to bed angry at someone; work out your differences.*

b. What does unresolved conflict do to a relationship? *(p. 23)*

*Answer: It builds walls of pain and bitterness which block communication and true understanding. An unresolved conflict is like a low-grade infection which can plague a relationship for years, even decades.*

2. How do parents' unresolved conflicts affect children? *(p. 23)*

*Possible Answer: Children aren't shown a positive way to resolve conflicts. They also might think the unresolved conflict is somehow their fault and could even try to resolve it themselves. An underlying current of tension in the home can make children feel insecure.*

3. What did you learn from your parents about handling conflict—good or bad? *(p. 23)*

*Tip: You might want to share from your own experience or perhaps call on someone whom you know well and who would be willing to share something they learned.*

*Read aloud* **HomeBuilders Principle #2: Unresolved conflict creates a potent acid which eats away at a marriage and family.**

### CONSTRUCTION
(10 minutes)

*This* **Construction** *project helps a couple begin talking to each other about the conflicts in their relationship.*

1. Go through the sections we've just completed.

2. What do you think are some common sources of conflict in your relationship?

a. _____

b. _____

31

c. _____

d. _____

e. _____

*Tip: State how much time couples have to talk. Point out that they will not have adequate time to fully explore the question.*

*As couples talk, announce when one minute is left. Have them conclude their time together by signing the personal pledge statement.*

3. Conclude your time together by reading the following personal pledge statement:

> "I pledge to you that I will use the next six weeks of this HomeBuilders study to build, strengthen, and encourage our marriage. I will make this study a priority in my schedule by faithfully keeping our 'dates,' working through the projects, and participating in the group discussions. You have my word on it."
>
> _____          _____
> (signed )                           (date)

Will you honor your mate by making this pledge your special commitment to him or her for the coming weeks? If so, sign your name in the space provided in *your mate's* study guide to document your commitment.

### BLUEPRINTS (continued)
(10–15 minutes)

> *This **Blueprints** section is designed to help couples explore scriptural guidelines for dealing positively with conflict in a relationship.*

## C. Pursuing Peace

Though conflict is inevitable, it is not God's ideal. God desires that we experience the peace and unity in a married relationship that we long for.

1. Read the following passages:

> Who is the man who desires life, and loves length of days that he may see good? Keep your tongue from evil, and your lips from speaking deceit. Depart from evil, and do good; seek peace, and pursue it. (Psalm 34:12–14)
>
> So then let us pursue the things which make for peace and the building up of one another. (Romans 14:19)

a. Why do you think God places so much importance on "living in peace"? *(p. 25)*

*Answer: He is the source of peace and has provided it for His people. He wants them to experience the wonderful benefits of His life in them.*

b. According to these passages, what are some things that you can do to maintain peace in your marriage? *(p. 25)*

*Answer: Seek peace, pursue things that make for peace, and decide to set my mind on God, the Source of peace.*

2. John 14:27 tells us that peace comes from God. Jesus said to His followers on their last evening together, "Peace I leave with you; My peace I give to you; not as the world gives, do I give to you." *(p. 26)*

a. Based on Jesus' example, what do you think God's peace is like? *(p. 26)*

*Answer: A kind of calm under pressure. Not always being in a hurry. Being aware of what is happening around us and yet not being hassled by it. Different than the world's peace, which almost always comes after the difficulty is over—not in the midst of difficulties.*

b. Why is it futile to try to achieve lasting peace with your mate apart from God? *(p. 26)*

*Answer: In order for peace to be real and lasting, it must come out of a peaceful heart. Only God can set the heart at peace.*

c. How do you go about finding God's peace in your life?" *(p. 26)*

*Answer: By developing a solid relationship with Him. Prayer is the key component of this relationship; as Philippians 4:7 says, you'll experience God's peace as you make your requests known to Him.*

*Read aloud* **HomeBuilders Principle #3: A peaceful relationship with your mate is possible when you pursue God's peace in your life.**

3. While pursuing peace and resolving conflict in a marriage is important, it needs to be done the right way.

   a. How have you seen conflict "resolved" the wrong way? *(p. 26)*

   _____

   _____

   b. What happens when a person pursues peace on the surface while burying bitterness and resentment? (p. 26)

   *Answer: The peace is temporary and superficial. Eventually the problem will burst into the open.*

   c. How do people who love a "good, healthy argument" often make the conflict worse? (p. 27)

   *Answer: They sometimes force an argument on their spouse when the spouse is not ready for it. Also, they are sometimes insensitive in what they say during the argument.*

**D. Reflection**

1. What is one thing you have learned from this session that you want to apply at home? (p. 27)

   _____

   _____

2. What do you hope to gain from the rest of this study? (p. 27)

_____

_____

*Have someone read aloud the following paragraph:*

As you can see, the Bible has much to offer to help you work through conflict. In the remaining sessions, you'll learn some practical concepts about transparency, listening, confronting, forgiving, and returning a blessing for an insult.

## MAKE A DATE

> *Each **HomeBuilders Project** is absolutely essential for couples to do together during the week. Emphasize that this is not home-work to earn a passing grade, but a highly significant time of interaction that will improve communication and understanding about effective conflict resolution.*
>
> *This first project is designed to build a couple's awareness of their typical responses to conflict and the quality of communication in their relationship.*

*Ask each couple to look at the **Make a Date** section of the study guide, and to agree on a time this week to complete **HomeBuilders Project #1** to-gether. Persuade couples to set aside 45 minutes to an hour to respond to the items individually and discuss their answers together.*

*Point out that the questions start out fairly nonthreatening, but quickly fo-cus on potentially sensitive issues. The intention is not to start arguments, but to stimulate honest reflection and interaction. While not every question will affect every couple in the same way, the time spent thinking and talk-ing will be more than worthwhile for any couple.*

*Remind the group that at the next session you will ask each couple to share one thing they discovered or discussed during the **HomeBuilders Project**. Also, remind group members to bring their calendars to the next session as an aid in scheduling their next date with their mates.*

## RECOMMENDED READING

> *The books listed at the end of each session are not required, but are recommended to reinforce and expand the concepts dealt with in the group session. Encourage couples to locate this book and read all or part of it before the next session. One effective idea is for one spouse to read aloud to the other, either in the morning before going to work or in the evening before retiring.*

**The Secret of Staying in Love,** by John Powell.
John Powell explains how we can nurture and strengthen loving relationships through the "secret" of staying in love: communication. He details the process of dialogue in simple exercises that give us a new and deeper knowledge of ourselves and those we love.

*Dismiss in prayer, or invite group members to volunteer one-sentence prayers focused on the challenges of effective conflict resolution.*

*Invite everyone to enjoy a time of fellowship and refreshments.*

## HOMEBUILDERS PROJECT #1

### Individually: 15 minutes

Write out your answers to the following questions:

1. When you have conflict in your marriage, how does it affect you?

_____

_____

2. If you have children, how does conflict between you and your mate affect them?

_____

_____

3. As you look at how you and your mate relate to each other, how would you rate your effectiveness in handling conflict? Circle the number on the following scale you think most applies to your marriage:

| 1 | 2 | 3 | 4 | 5 |
|---|---|---|---|---|
| ineffective | | | | very effective |

4. What is one thing you appreciate about how your mate handles conflict in your marriage?

_____

_____

5. Many people withdraw from conflict; others pursue it. Which do you do, and why?

_____

_____

6. If you could change one thing about how you and your mate handle conflict, what it would be?

_____

_____

**Interact As a Couple: 30–45 minutes**

1. If you didn't have enough time to talk during the **Construction** project, take some more time now. It's important to pinpoint differences which will naturally lead to conflict.

2. Discuss the questions you answered during your individual time.

3. List three things that you can start doing now to improve how you handle conflict as a couple.

　a. _____

b. _____

c. _____

4. Commit yourself to put those three ideas into action for at least one week.

Remember to bring your calendar for **Make a Date** to the next session.

# SESSION TWO
*Transparency*

## FOCUS

Resolving conflict begins as we understand
each other through transparency.

## Objectives

You will help your group members understand the concept of transparent communication as you guide them to:

■ Define the term *transparency* and describe its benefits in a relationship;

■ Rate the levels of communication in their marriages; and

■ Discuss methods to improve transparency in their communication.

## Overall Comments

1. In Session Two, couples are asked to evaluate their level of transparency. Many couples fall into a pattern of sharing very little of their real selves with each other. Often this pattern results from the time pressures of job and family commitments. Sometimes couples may realize their communication is lacking but need an impetus to consciously begin the process of open sharing and self-disclosure. Success in a marriage is more than just peaceful coexistence. The goal toward which God intends us to strive is that of two people sharing and growing as individuals and as a couple. The potential benefits of transparency in marriage give an exciting dimension to living as a couple.

2. Be sure that each individual has a study guide. Husbands and wives will be asked to complete parts of the **Construction** project individually.

## WARM UP
(15–20 minutes)

> *The **Warm Up** involves consideration of a statement by Swiss psychiatrist Paul Tournier from his book,* To Understand Each Other. *Couples then talk about the pros and cons of being known intimately by another. Your comments and your mate's will set the tone for the level of openness the group is able to establish.*

*Greet people warmly as they arrive. Engage them in informal conversation about events of the week until it is time to begin.*

*Start the session on time, even if not everyone is present yet.*

*Ask for a show of hands of the couples who kept their date with each other and completed the first **HomeBuilders Project**. Affirm those who did so.*

1. *Invite volunteers to share insights gained during their private time together.* Begin this session by sharing one thing you learned from **HomeBuilders Project #1.** *(p. 34)*

2. Read the following quote *(p. 34)*:

   *Note: Read the quote aloud to the group members.*

   > No one comes to know himself through introspection, or in the solitude of his personal diary. He who would see himself clearly must open up to a confidant freely chosen and worthy of trust.
   >
   > Dr. Paul Tournier

   Most likely your mate knows more about you than anyone else. What is the best part of being known in this way by him/her? *(p. 34)*

   ***Possible Answers:*** *Comfort, security, familiarity, trust, etc.*

   ***Tip:*** *Invite group members to mention the benefits of having a mate know the deep, personal side of one's life.*

3. What is the worst part about being known in this way by your mate? *(p. 34)*

**Possible Answers:** *Worry about whether he/she will still love and admire, possible boredom, knowledge may be used as a weapon, etc.*

## BLUEPRINTS
(20–30 minutes)

> *The purpose of this* **Blueprints** *section is to help couples understand the concept and purpose of transparency in marriage.*

## A. The Need for Transparency

The word *transparency* is often used to describe two people who are committed to each other, who trust each other and thus are able to know each other well.

Not all people want to be transparent with one another. In fact, many feel that being transparent is one of the greatest risks they can take.

1. As a group, select three words that you think are most descriptive of the word *transparency*. In what ways can these words, applied to two people, help a marriage?" *(p. 35)*

   **Possible Answers:** *openness, honesty, trust*

2. Why is it difficult for some people to be transparent with another person? *(p. 35)*

   **Answer:** *They may not have an outgoing personality. They may have grown up in homes where transparency was not encouraged. They may be fearful of rejection.*

3. Why is it often harder for men to be transparent than it is for women (especially when it comes to admitting their need for their wives)? *(p. 36)*

   **Answer:** *In our culture, men are not always encouraged to be open and honest, particularly about feelings.*

41

4. Most people marry with the hope of being transparent, of openly sharing their thoughts and feelings with each other. In what ways is this hope of transparency damaged in so many relationships? *(p. 36)*

*Answer: The hope is damaged when a spouse loses interest, gets too busy, criticizes his or her mate, unwisely shares secrets about his or her mate with a friend, etc.*

5. Why do couples need transparency in marriage? *(p. 36)*

*Answer: True intimacy and oneness in marriage requires it.*

## B. Transparency Demands Openness

Communication takes place in varying degrees of openness. The descriptions and chart that follow help show where transparency fits in the communication continuum. All of these levels of communication are used to some extent in every marriage.

1. LEVEL ONE: Cliché communication allows one to remain safely isolated and alone. It is restricted to greetings and comments which express no opinions, feelings, or real information.

   What's an example of cliché communication? *(p. 36)*

   *Possible Answers: "Hi, how are you?" "Oh, fine. And you?" "Fine."*

2. LEVEL TWO: Fact communication consists only of the objective discussion of facts. Gossip or data analysis holds others at arm's length.

   Share an illustration of how this type of communication occurred in your family this week. *(p. 37)*

3. LEVEL THREE: Opinion communication involves sharing ideas and opinions. People who communicate on this level open up enough to express what they really think.

4. LEVEL FOUR: Emotional communication involves sharing feelings and emotions leading to complete communication. It involves conveying one's hopes, fears, likes, dislikes, aspirations, disappointments, joys, sorrows, needs, dreams, failures, desires, stresses, sources of fulfillment, discouragements, and burdens.

5. LEVEL FIVE: Transparent communication involves complete emotional and personal truthfulness. Transparency is sharing your heart with another person.

Why is this level of communication one which you should only share with a few people? *(p. 37)*

*Answer: First, this type of communication requires a great deal of time and commitment, and you probably won't be able to give that to very many people. Second, you should reserve a special level of intimacy and transparency for your marriage relationship.*

## CONSTRUCTION
### (10 minutes)

---

*This **Construction** project helps a couple evaluate the levels of communication in their marriage. Growing from one level to the next is necessary for a successful marriage.*

---

*Instruct each couple to work individually on questions 1–3, then share with each other the completed evaluations.*

*As couples talk, announce when one minute is left.*

### Individually:

1. Using the information we have just discussed, evaluate how effectively you and your spouse communicate. Using a scale of 1–5, write the appropriate ratings in the chart:

| 1 | 2 | 3 | 4 | 5 |
|------|------|------|-----------|-----------|
| poor | fair | good | very good | excellent |

| Communication Level | Meaning | Rating (1–5) |
|---|---|---|
| LEVEL ONE: Cliché | Nonsharing | _____ |
| LEVEL TWO: Fact | Sharing what you know | _____ |
| LEVEL THREE: Opinion | Sharing what you think | _____ |
| LEVEL FOUR: Emotion | Sharing what you feel | _____ |
| LEVEL FIVE: Transparency | Sharing who you are | _____ |

2. What is one step you could take to achieve greater transparency?

_____

_____

3. What is one step you think your mate could take to achieve greater transparency?

_____

_____

**Interact As a Couple:**

Share your conclusions with each other.

### BLUEPRINTS (continued)
(15–30 minutes)

*This **Blueprints** section is designed to help couples become more aware of some hindrances to transparency within a marriage. Fear of criticism or unwanted advice often inhibits self-disclosure. In contrast, responsible, loving transparency creates a climate in which an individual and a couple can overcome weaknesses.*

### C. Four Steps toward Transparency

*Tip: This section of the study will be a time for each group member to reflect silently on the four steps suggested. Begin by commenting on the importance of the first step. This is a good place to briefly share how your personal relationship with Christ affords you transparency before Him. Then ask all to silently and thoughtfully review the four steps given. After a few moments, instruct them to then move on to the reflection.*

1. STEP ONE: Begin by being open with God.

   a. King David, when trying to rectify relationships, was first transparent with God. Read what he wrote in the Psalms:

   > Search me, O God, and know my heart; try me and know my anxious thoughts; and see if there be any hurtful way in me, and lead me in the everlasting way. (Psalm 139: 23–24)

   Do you find this type of transparency with God difficult or easy? Why? *(p. 40)*

   _____

   _____

   b. As you think of being transparent with your mate, why is this first step of utmost importance? *(p. 40)*

   *Answer: Openness with God reduces a person's pride, thus allowing him/her to be open and vulnerable with another.*

   *Tip: This would be a good place for you as the leader to illustrate this principle from your own married life.*

2. STEP TWO: Commit to create an atmosphere of love, commitment, and forgiveness in your home. *(p. 41)*

   a. Read the following verse: "There is no fear in love; but perfect love casts out fear" (1 John 4:18).

   All of us, if we will admit it, have some fears of being known for who we really are. How does fear affect transparency? *(p. 41)*

   *Answer: If you fear that another person will judge you, you won't be transparent with him or her.*

   How can love "cast out fear"? *(p. 41)*

   *Answer: If you know your mate loves you unconditionally and will not judge you for admitting faults and failures, you feel free to be transparent.*

b. Read the following passage:

> For this cause a man shall leave his father and his mother, and shall cleave to his wife; and they shall become one flesh. And the man and his wife were both naked and were not ashamed. (Genesis 2:24–25)

The word *cleave* carries the suggestion of total commitment. When the two of you stood before parents, friends, and relatives on your wedding day, you committed to "have and to hold from this day forward . . . ," in spite of the incredible pressures that were sure to come.

How does your total commitment enable your mate to be transparent? *(p. 41)*

*Answer: When you express and act out your total commitment to your mate—to love and accept, no matter what, and to help him/her grow spiritually—your mate will feel the freedom to be transparent and admit struggles.*

c. Read the following passage:

> Let all bitterness and wrath and anger and clamor and slander be put away from you, along with all malice. And be kind to one another, tender-hearted, forgiving each other, just as God in Christ also has forgiven you. (Ephesians 4:31–32)

If you express forgiveness freely and regularly, how does this help your mate be transparent with you? *(p. 42)*

*Answer: Expressing forgiveness is like building a mirror of transparency—what you do to your spouse is reflected by him/her back to you.*

*Note:* We have only briefly touched on the subject of forgiveness here, but because of its importance in relationships we have devoted an entire session to it later in the study.

*Read aloud* **HomeBuilders Principle #4: Love, commitment, and forgiveness provide the environment for a person to be willing to be known by another.**

3. STEP THREE: Affirm your mate when he or she practices transparency.

Why is it important for you to affirm and acknowledge your mate's efforts when they occur? *(p. 42)*

**Answer:** *Because then your mate will be more willing to be transparent in the future; affirmation increases your mate's confidence in himself/ herself and in you.*

4. STEP FOUR: Pray with one another regularly.

How does praying together openly and honestly promote transparency and intimacy? If you can, share an experience in which this occurred. *(p. 42)*

**Answer:** *True prayer requires humility and also promotes humility. And humility will lead to great transparency because you won't feel the need to hide anything from your mate.*

---

---

## D. Stifling Transparency

1. Read through the following case study:

*Note: Call on a group member to read the case study aloud.*

### CASE STUDY

Anne is having trouble at her office with Melissa, one of her associates. She confides her frustration to her husband, who replies, "You absolutely must get rid of Melissa. Stand up for yourself, or she will walk right over you! How many times have I told you already: you're too weak, too easy on your people? I wouldn't let her get away with these things. Go and report this to the management!"

a. What has Anne's husband done to stifle her attempt at being transparent with him? *(p. 43)*

   **Answer:** *Criticize her; compare her with himself.*

   **Tip:** *Invite the wives to share how they would feel after hearing this husband's response.*

b. To what level of communication (see chart in **Construction** section) will she likely resort during future encounters with him? *(p. 43)*

   **Answer:** *Cliché or fact communication.*

c. Read Ephesians 4:29:

   > Let no unwholesome word proceed from your mouth, but only such a word as is good for edification according to the need of the moment, that it may give grace to those who hear.

   Write a more appropriate response that Anne's husband could have given, following the advice in Ephesians 4:29. *(p. 43)*

---

2. Read the following passages from the Book of Proverbs:

   > When there are many words, transgression is unavoidable, but he who restrains his lips is wise. (Proverbs 10:19)

   > There is one who speaks rashly like the thrusts of a sword, but the tongue of the wise brings healing. (Proverbs 12:18)

   > The one who guards his mouth preserves his life; the one who opens wide his lips comes to ruin. (Proverbs 13:3)

   **Tip:** *Assign each couple one of the Scripture verses in the study guide. Instruct them to confer with each other about what responsibilities their passage describes. After a few moments, encourage couples to share their insights about the verses they read.*

   a. What counsel do these Proverbs offer to you as you seek to be more transparent with your mate? *(p. 44)*

*Answer: It is possible to be too transparent. Even as you seek to be honest with your mate, ask God for wisdom in what to say and what not to say. Some people, all in the name of "being honest," have actually hurt their mates and damaged the trust level in their relationships by sharing certain accusations and feelings and confessions.*

b. Some marriage relationships have been damaged when people tell friends about things their mates have shared with them in confidence. How can you maintain your mate's trust? *(p. 44)*

*Answer: By guarding your tongue and not telling others what your mate tells you in confidence.*

Read aloud **HomeBuilders Principle #5: To enjoy the privileges of transparency, you need to control the power of the tongue.**

### E. Reflection

1. What is one thing you have learned from this session that you want to apply in your life? *(p. 44)*

_____

_____

### MAKE A DATE

> *Each **HomeBuilders Project** is absolutely essential for couples to do together during the week. This week, couples will spend time evaluating their level of transparency with one another as they seek to share their needs for understanding.*

*Ask each couple to look at the **Make a Date** section of the study guide, then agree on a time this week to complete **HomeBuilders Project #2** together. Persuade couples to set aside 45 minutes to an hour to respond to the items individually and then discuss their answers.*

*Remind the group that at the next session you will ask each couple to share one thing they discovered or discussed during their **HomeBuilders Project**.*

*Also, remind group members to bring their calendars to the next session as an aid in scheduling their next date with their mates.*

## RECOMMENDED READING

> *The reading is not required, but is highly recommended to reinforce and expand the concepts dealt with in the group session. Encourage couples to locate this book and to read all or part of it before the next session. One effective idea is for one person to read aloud to the other, either in the morning before going to work or in the evening before retiring.*

**To Understand Each Other**, by Paul Tournier.

The ability to understand each other is what counts in working out marital happiness together. With wisdom and warmth, Swiss psychiatrist Paul Tournier suggests ways to achieve this understanding.

*Dismiss in prayer, or invite group members to volunteer one-sentence prayers focused on the need for better communication in their marriages. Then invite everyone to enjoy a time of fellowship and refreshments.*

## HOMEBUILDERS PROJECT #2

**Individually: 20 minutes**

1. In what ways has the love and understanding provided by your mate helped you be more transparent? Think of some specific instances.

 

 

2. Describe a recent situation in which your transparency was stifled either by criticism or by advice from your mate. Tell how that made you feel about being transparent again on that particular subject.

 

 

3. Go through the "Four Steps Toward Transparency" in the **Blueprints** section. What practical steps can you take to begin creating an atmosphere in which you are free to be transparent? Write out an action plan.

_____

_____

_____

_____

_____

_____

**Interact As a Couple: 25 minutes**

1. Read to each other your responses from your individual time in this **HomeBuilders Project.** Allow these to be read without comment.

2. Talk together about your mutual need for understanding in the areas where transparency may be stifled.

3. Discuss your action plans. What specific steps do you need to take to encourage transparency in your marriage?

_____

_____

_____

_____

_____

4. Pray together for sensitivity and loving understanding in future communication times.

Remember to bring your calendar for **Make a Date** to the next session.

# The HomeBuilders

## COUPLES SERIES

"Unless the Lord builds the house,
they labor in vain who build it."
Psalm 127:1

## SESSION THREE
*Listening*

## FOCUS

Resolution of conflict
requires a commitment to listen.

## Objectives

You will help your group members improve their communication skills in
conflict situations as you guide them to:

■ Evaluate the listening habits of a couple in a case study;

■ Identify good and bad listening habits; and

■ Select and practice several good listening habits.

## Overall Comments

Session Three provides a foundation for conflict resolution by promoting good
listening habits. TV sitcoms, contemporary movies, and even our own family
backgrounds often illustrate the consequences of poor listening. Communication patterns formed over the years can only be transformed as a couple becomes
aware of godly principles for relating to one another. Establishing good listening habits is a valuable asset to a couple striving for a successful marriage.

## WARM UP
(15–20 minutes)

*Sometimes the very act of discussing how to handle conflict
causes couples to experience strife! This **Warm Up** includes an
optional question (here in the leader's guide only) which will
allow you to ask about this possibility.*

*Greet people warmly as they arrive. Be aware of group members who may not yet have built any relationships with other couples. Initiate friendly conversations with these people, then involve another couple in the conversation with you. Start the session on time, even if not everyone is present yet.*

*Begin the session by asking which couples kept their date with each other and completed last week's **HomeBuilders Project**. Affirm those who did so.*

*Share one insight you gained from your time with your mate. Then invite volunteers to share similarly from their interaction in the **HomeBuilders Project** by referring to question 1:*

1. Begin this session by sharing one thing you learned from **HomeBuilders Project #2**. *(p. 50)*

---
---

***Optional Question #1:*** *Ask, "Has there been any increase in conflict between you since we began this study?" If any couples answer affirmatively, ask, "Why do you think this is occurring?" **Answer:** Talking about conflict tends to unearth unresolved strife—areas that we've ignored or avoided discussing in the past. Assure the couples that this type of conflict is natural and that they are not the only ones who have experienced this. Also, mention that resolution of conflict is better in the long haul than avoidance.*

***Optional Question #2:*** *Bring the following four objects with you to the session and pick up or point to each: TV set, Bible, tennis/walking shoes, and a telephone. Ask, "What do these four things have in common?" **Answer:** Each has something to do with words, listening, and time. Some will want to know how the shoes fit in with the other three. Suggest that sometimes we have to get away from the TV and phone in order to be able to talk without interruption, and that walking together is one way to do that. This is a subtle suggestion that walking together may be a good way of resolving conflict through listening.*

2. During this session we will talk about listening. What are some ways you can tell if a person is not listening to you when you are talking? *(p. 50)*

*Possible Answer: Lack of eye contact, interruptions in mid-sentence, etc.*

3. Complete this statement: "When another person isn't listening to me, the thing that bothers me most is _____

_____." *(p. 50)*

## BLUEPRINTS
(20 minutes)

> *This Blueprints section introduces several poor listening habits and some of the negative results of these habits.*

If we don't hear one another, we can't achieve understanding. And without understanding, it's impossible to resolve conflict. So becoming a good listener is a key step toward resolving conflict and opening the lines of communication.

### A. Poor Listening Habits Fuel Conflict

*Choose an animated couple from the group to be Brian and Linda in the following scenario. Play the part of the moderator yourself. Ask everyone else to close their books while the skit is presented.*

*After the skit, lead the group in responding to the four questions posed in the study guide.*

SKIT
The Consequences of Poor Listening

MODERATOR: It has been a long, trying Monday for both Brian and his wife, Linda. Fall is Brian's favorite time of year because of his love for professional football, and Monday night is his favorite night of the week. Linda enjoys an occasional game as well and has joined him in the family room. The end of the day and the smell of hot popcorn promises a pleasant evening at home together—or does it?

LINDA: "Brian, I wonder why our new neighbors always leave their garage door open. Wouldn't you think they would be afraid of someone stealing their things?"

BRIAN: "I don't know."

LINDA: "I was thinking . . . we need to have them over sometime. I wonder if they know anyone around here. Maybe next weekend we could invite them and some of our friends over for a barbecue."

BRIAN: "Uh-huh."

LINDA (sarcastically): "I can tell you are really concerned about these people, Brian."

BRIAN: "Hmmmm."

LINDA: "Your mom called yesterday, honey. She says that all your dad wants for his birthday this year is another TV set—for the bathroom. Can you imagine, Brian, a TV set in the bathroom?"

BRIAN: "What kind does he want?"

LINDA: "You're just like your dad! If you had TV in the bathroom you'd never come out—and you're in there too long as it is."

BRIAN: "Would you mind getting some salt for the popcorn, Linda?"

LINDA (a little heated): "You get your own salt!"

BRIAN: "Now wait a minute! You know I don't want to miss any of this game. Now get the salt!"

LINDA (sarcastically): "I think it would be all right for you to miss just a little of the game. You certainly have missed a lot of this conversation."

BRIAN (with strong emotion): "Look, I'm not in this room to be talking. Do I have to take this TV set into the bathroom to watch this game? Maybe I will go in there—at least I won't be interrupted!"

LINDA (sarcastically): "Fine! Shall I slip the salt under the door, or do you want to come out during a commercial?"

1. What poor listening habits are Brian and Linda exhibiting? *(p. 52)*

   *Answer: Brian's poor listening habits include pseudo-listening, which fakes interest; selective listening, which tunes in only for points of interest; and protective listening, which doesn't hear any threatening messages, then is surprised by the explosion. Linda is not listening well, either, because she's trying to force her husband to listen to her at a time when he is not willing.*

2. How do poor listening habits make an argument worse than it needs to be? *(p. 52)*

   *Answer: If you aren't actively listening to your mate, you can magnify an argument by misinterpreting what he or she is saying or by missing part of the message. In addition, not listening in itself may irritate your mate and escalate the anger level in the argument.*

3. If you were Brian, how could you listen to your wife better and still enjoy the evening's game? *(p. 52)*

   *Answer: Brian could have lovingly mentioned that he can't listen to two things at the same time. Perhaps he could suggest that they talk during the commercials, when he would turn off the sound, or that they would set aside time later to talk. Also, he needs to assure her that football is not first in his life, but rather that this game is important at this time.*

4. If you were Linda, what could you have done to get your husband to talk with you more? *(p. 53)*

   *Answer: Linda's best option would have been to pick another time for this conversation. Second, she could have accepted the signs of Brian's inattention without using them as ammunition against him. Instead of drawing him into dialogue, she drove him further from it.*

5. Can you recall an argument between you and your mate that was aggravated by your poor listening? Share it with the group. *(p. 53)*

 

6. Read the following Proverbs *(p. 53)*:

> He who gives an answer before he hears, it is folly and shame to him. (Proverbs 18:13)

> A fool finds no pleasure in understanding but delights in airing his own opinions. (Proverbs 18:2, NIV)

What guidance do these verses provide for:

a. Brian and Linda?

 

b. You?

 

## CONSTRUCTION
(10–15 minutes)

> *This **Construction** project gives each couple an opportunity to evaluate and discuss their own listening habits.*

*Instruct each couple to work through the material individually, then share their answers with their mates.*

**Individually:**

1. How would you evaluate yourself as a listener? For each question below, circle the response that is most true of you.*

---

\* These questions reprinted by permission from H. Norman Wright, *Communication: Key to Your Marriage,* (Ventura, Calif.: Regal Books, 1974), pp. 56–57.

a. As your mate talks to you, do you find it difficult to keep your mind from wandering to other things?

       Yes          No          Sometimes

b. When your mate talks, do you go beyond the facts being discussed and try to sense how he or she is feeling about the matter?

       Yes          No          Sometimes

c. Do certain words or phrases your mate uses tend to prejudice you so that you cannot objectively listen to what is being said?

       Yes          No          Sometimes

d. When you are puzzled or annoyed by what your mate says, do you try to get the questions straightened out as soon as possible?

       Yes          No          Sometimes

e. If you feel it would take a lot of time and effort to understand something, do you go out of your way to avoid hearing about it?

       Yes          No          Sometimes

f. When your mate talks to you, do you try to make him or her think you are paying attention when you are not?

       Yes          No          Sometimes

g. When you are listening to your mate, are you easily distracted by outside sights and sounds (such as the TV set, someone walking by, music, the kids, etc.)?

       Yes          No          Sometimes

2. Now evaluate your mate as a listener. For each of the seven questions listed above, place an "X" over the response most true of him/her.

## Interact As a Couple:

Take a few minutes to discuss your answers with each other.

*Note: As couples talk, announce when one minute is left.*

### BLUEPRINTS (continued)
(20–30 minutes)

> *This **Blueprints** section is planned to help couples examine scriptural truths for proper listening. The first two questions consider the significance of listening to God. The third provides opportunity to see the values of listening on an interpersonal level.*

## B. Listening Helps Defuse Conflict

1. What did you learn about yourself and your mate during the **Construction** project? How can you use that information to improve your communication? *(p. 56)*

   *Tip: Use this question to guide couples in sharing what they learned during their **Construction** project.*

2. What are some of the benefits of being a good listener? List as many as you can. *(p. 56)*

   *Answer: It helps your mate trust you. It makes him feel important and wanted. It helps him want to open up to you.*

3. When your mate really listens to you, how do you feel? In what ways does your mate's listening build you up? *(p. 56)*

   _____

   _____

4. Read James 1:19: "Let everyone be quick to hear, slow to speak . . ." *(p. 57)*

a. What would happen in most of your marital conflicts if you applied this principle? *(p. 57)*

*Answer: Many of them would be resolved, because many conflicts are rooted in the problem that people speak too much and listen too little.*

b. Think of a recent example in which you as a couple applied this truth and were drawn together because of it. *(p. 57)*

---

---

*Tip: Ask everyone to read James 1:19 out loud together. Then, read it together once more, emphasizing the words* quick *and* slow. *Invite discussion about what would happen if this principle were applied in their conflicts. Instruct everyone to privately jot down a time or two when they did it right—applied this principle and listened first. After a minute or two of thinking and writing, solicit volunteers who will relate one of those experiences and what made them "quick to listen." Be prepared to share an incident from your own marriage to stimulate their memory and help them feel comfortable telling their story.*

*Read aloud* **HomeBuilders Principle #6: A commitment to becoming a better listener will help you avoid many conflicts, and will also help you resolve others before they grow too difficult.**

## C. Becoming a Good Listener

*Tip: The following three steps will help drive home what has been discussed and lend practical application to the topic of becoming better listeners.*

1. STEP ONE: Maintain a teachable heart.

a. What happens to communication if you are not teachable? *(p. 57)*

b. Read the following passages:

> A wise man will hear and increase in learning. (Proverbs 1:5 )

Incline your ear and come to Me. Listen, that you may live.
(Isaiah 55:3)

How can listening to God help you become a better listener with your mate? *(p. 58)*

**Answer:** *A heart kept soft by listening to the Lord is a heart that hears other people as well.*

**Tip:** *Remind group members of the need to listen regularly to God through His Word in order for the heart to remain soft and teachable.*

*Invite the ones in your group who faithfully spend time in God's Word to share what has been most helpful to them in building consistency in listening to God. (But be careful that this doesn't lend a "better than you" mood to the sharing. Point out (if it is true) that these people (those who listen to God) also tend to be good listeners to other people. Ask what connection there might be.*

2. STEP TWO: Give your mate focused attention.

Focused attention involves several elements:

▸  Picking the proper time and place.

▸  Making sure there are no distractions.

▸  Maintaining eye contact.

▸  Allowing enough time to work through the conflict.

a. What have you found to be good times and places for talking about important subjects or working through conflict with your mate? *(p. 58)*

_____

_____

b. What are some poor times and places? *(p. 58)*

_____

_____

3. STEP THREE: Commit to understanding your mate.

Good listening requires more than focusing on what the person is saying. Your goal is truly to understand what your mate thinks, wants, and feels.

> Each one speaks primarily in order to set forth his own ideas. Exceedingly few exchanges of viewpoints manifest a real desire to understand the other person.
> Dr. Paul Tournier

> You husbands . . . live with your wives in an understanding way. (1 Peter 3:7)

a. What important things do you do to ensure that you understand what your mate is saying? *(p. 59)*

---

---

***Tip:*** *Be prepared to suggest some possibilities here. Also point out that this week's **HomeBuilders Project** will suggest a method for enhancing listening.*

b. Stop for a couple of minutes and think of a time when God has given you greater understanding about a conflict with your mate because you took the time to listen to him or her. If you can, share about this experience with the group. *(p. 59)*

---

---

***Tip:*** *Be prepared for you or your spouse to share an example from your own marriage.*

## D. Reflection

***Tip:*** *Allow the time for each of the following questions to be answered. Remind the group that all the biblical passages in this session are to be considered as they answer question #1.*

1. Look back over this session and select the scripture that was most meaningful to you. Why did you choose this passage? *(p 59)*

_____

_____

2. What is one thing you have learned from this session that you want to apply to your life? *(p. 59)*

_____

_____

## MAKE A DATE

*Each **HomeBuilders Project** is essential for couples to do together during the week. This week's interaction will improve couples' listening skills in dealing with real areas of conflict.*

*Ask each couple to look at the **Make a Date** section of the study guide, then agree on a time this week to complete **HomeBuilders Project #3** together.*

*Call attention to the phrases which are suggested for use in clarifying areas of potential misunderstanding. Most people will feel awkward trying to fit these into a discussion, but after a time or two, these phrases will begin to feel natural and will prove their value.*

*Remind the group that at the next session you will ask each couple to share one thing they discovered or discussed during their **HomeBuilders Project**. Also, remind group members to bring their calendars to the next session as an aid in scheduling their next date with their mates.*

## RECOMMENDED READING

*Encourage couples to locate the books listed in their study guides and read the recommended chapters before the next session.*

**Communication: Key to Your Marriage** (chapters 4 and 9), by H. Norman Wright.

In this book, Dr. Wright's ideas are ready to help you not just talk about communication, but do it effectively. Learn more than a dozen ways to cope with marital conflict, plus ten practical principles for building your partner's self-esteem through understanding and respect, ten methods for handling angry feelings, and ten steps to avoiding the high cost of anxiety and worry.

**Achieving the Impossible: Intimate Marriage** (chapter 6), by Charles M. Sell.

In this book, Dr. Sell reveals the principles that will allow you to make individual differences work for your marriage, to face and handle conflicts, to deal with life's inevitable crises, to develop intimacy, and to be a caring listener.

*Dismiss in prayer, or invite group members to volunteer one-sentence prayers focused on the challenges of effective conflict resolution.*

*Invite everyone to enjoy a time of fellowship and refreshments.*

## HOMEBUILDERS PROJECT #3

**Individually: 10–15 minutes**

1. Review the entire **Blueprints** section.

2. What do you think are your mate's strengths and weaknesses when it comes to listening?

_____

_____

3. What are your own strengths and weaknesses when it comes to listening?

_____

_____

4. What are some practical steps you can take to become a better listener?

_____

_____

5. Summarize your desire to become a better listener by writing a brief pledge to your mate, in 50 words or less. Make it from the heart:

_____

_____

_____

_____

_____

_____

_____

**Interact As a Couple: 30–40 minutes**

1. Select an area of current conflict between the two of you (children, stepchildren, finances, a purchase, in-laws, schedule, social event, etc.).

2. HUSBAND: Take 5–10 minutes to give your point of view about the above issue while your wife listens without comment.

   WIFE: When your husband is finished, repeat to him what you heard by using one or all of the following phrases:

   ▶ "What I understand you to say is . . ."

   ▶ "Do I understand you to mean . . .?"

   ▶ "You may not have meant this, but what I heard you say is . . ."

   Allow him to clear up any misunderstood communication, but at this point, don't make a specific effort to resolve the conflict. Simply allow your mate to speak to a listening ear.

3. Now, switch roles. WIFE: Explain your viewpoint. HUSBAND: Repeat to her what she just said, allowing her, too, to speak to a listening ear.

4. Of what value has this brief exercise in listening been to each of you?

---

---

5. Read to each other the pledges you wrote in question #5 of the individual section of this **HomeBuilders Project**. Talk together about how the two of you can build better listening habits.

6. Close your time together in prayer and commit before the Lord to listen to each other better.

Remember to bring your calendar for **Make a Date** to the next session.

# The HomeBuilders

## COUPLES SERIES

"Unless the Lord builds the house,
they labor in vain who build it."
Psalm 127:1

## SESSION FOUR
*Confronting*

## FOCUS

Loving confrontation
can help a relationship by offering
a way to practice real love.

## Objectives

In this session, you will help couples discern common methods of dealing with conflict and become aware of God's plan for conflict resolution as you guide them to:

■ Study ways in which Bible people dealt with conflicts;

■ Describe their own habitual styles of dealing with conflict; and

■ Discuss guidelines for dealing with conflict in a loving but truthful manner.

## Overall Comments

Session Four presents a discussion of a significant aspect of marital happiness—the importance of dealing appropriately with disagreements. Problem situations, both small and large, important and insignificant, can create havoc in a relationship. Confrontation, especially with family members or close friends, is a risky business. By examining biblical examples, it is possible to grasp some practical guidelines which help us reach our goal of healthy conflict resolution.

## WARM UP
(15–20 minutes)

*The **Warm Up** involves people in reflecting and sharing their responses to having mistakes pointed out to them. As people talk about the very human reactions to criticism, they will build a sense of common experiences which will aid them in being honest in the personal evaluations that follow.*

*Greet people individually as they arrive. Avoid the temptation to be busy with last-minute preparations. From the time the first couple enters, your attention needs to be focused on helping them feel glad they took the time to come.*

*Start the session on time, even if not everyone is present yet.*

*Ask for a show of hands of the couples who did not keep their date with each other to complete HomeBuilders Project #3. If there are any who failed to do the project, point out that this session deals with the importance of loving confrontation in a relationship. "I obviously want to maintain a positive relationship with everyone in the group, and I also want to encourage everyone to follow through on these projects. Perhaps this study will give me some tips on how to accomplish both those objectives as we explore ways to deal with problems and conflicts in our marriages."*

1. Begin this session by sharing one thing you learned from **HomeBuilders Project #3**. *(p. 62)*

   ***Tip:*** *Invite volunteers to share an insight gained from their interaction in the **HomeBuilders Project**.*

2. In any relationship, there are times when you must confront someone about a problem, a misunderstanding, a transgression, or even a bad or annoying habit. What are some good or bad ways of confronting that you have observed—among children, teenagers, parents, adults, etc.? *(p. 68)*

3. What are some ways people try to avoid confrontation? *(p. 68)*

   ***Answer:*** *They act as if the problem doesn't exist. They avoid the person they need to talk with.*

### BLUEPRINTS
(15–20 minutes)

> *This **Blueprints** section explains five common methods of conflict resolution then illustrates each with biblical examples.*

## A. Choices for Dealing with Conflict.

We have begun to learn that conflict can draw two people together by bringing greater understanding, or it can drive a wedge of resentment and fear between them. Most of us tend to avoid conflict because we have not been taught effective ways to face it.

1. There are four possible ways of dealing with conflict *(p. 69–70)*:

   **Fight to Win:** The "I win, you lose/I'm right, you're wrong" position. Domination is usually reflected in this style; personal relationships take second place to the need to triumph.

   **Withdraw:** The "I'm uncomfortable, so I'll get out" position. Viewing conflict as a hopeless inevitability kills the interest in even trying to work out a resolution. Personal relationships take second place to avoiding discomfort.

   **Yield:** The "Rather than start another argument, whatever you wish is fine" position. People who take this approach assume it is far better to be nice, to submit, to go along with the other's demands than to risk a confrontation. To them, a safe feeling is more important than a close relationship.

   **Lovingly Confront:** The "I care enough about you to deal with this issue as it really is" position. This approach offers the maximum possibility of satisfactory resolution with the minimum of threat and stress. The relationship is valued as higher than winning or losing, escaping, or feeling comfortable.

2. What is your usual style of handling conflict? *(p. 70)*

3. Has your style changed since you became a Christian? If so, how? *(p. 70)*

4. How do you think your style of handling conflict affects your mate? *(p. 70)*

## B. We Can Learn about Conflict from Real People

The Bible is filled with real people—people in conflict. Determine which of the four styles of dealing with conflict are exhibited in each of the following dramas:

1. Adam and Eve were discovered by God after eating the forbidden fruit.

   > Then the Lord God called to the man, and said to him, "Where are you?" And he [Adam] said, "I heard the sound of Thee in the garden, and I was afraid because I was naked; so I hid myself." (Genesis 3:9–10)

   a. How did Adam and Eve respond to this conflict with God?*(p. 71)*

   *Answer: Withdraw.*

   b. What are ways couples withdraw from each other in marriage? *(p. 71)*

   *Answer: They develop separate interests to avoid having to spend time with one another. They become unwilling to be transparent with each other or honest with themselves. They look to their children to have emotional needs met when they should be looking to their mate to fill those needs.*

2. Saul discovered that his son, Jonathan, was befriending young David, the object of the king's intense jealousy: "Then Saul hurled his spear at him to strike him down." (1 Samuel 20:33)

   a. What was Saul's style of handling conflict? *(p. 71)*

   *Answer: Fight to Win.*

   b. Why is this style so common in marriage? What are some "spears" that husbands and wives typically hurl at each other? *(p. 71)*

   *Answer: This style is common because most people don't know how to handle their hurt and anger in any other way. The most common "spears" are verbal ones.*

3. Pharaoh's officials spotted Abram and Sarai as they traveled in Egypt. Abram feared for his life, and he also knew that Pharaoh liked beautiful women:

   > And it came about when he came near to Egypt, that he said to Sarai his wife, "See now, I know that you are a beautiful woman;

and it will come about when the Egyptians see you, that they will say, 'This is his wife'; and they will kill me, but they will let you live. Please say that you are my sister so that it may go well with me because of you, and that I may live on account of you." (Genesis 12:11–13)

a. What was Abram's way of dealing with this conflict? *(p. 72)*

*Answer: Yield.*

b. How can yielding in a conflict and not confronting it truthfully make the conflict worse? *(p. 72)*

*Answer: Sometimes yielding seems the easy way out, because it defuses the immediate problem. But yielding can lead to bitterness. And the mate of a person who yields consistently often starts taking advantage of him/her.*

4. Both the Old and New Testaments depict examples of yet another style:

a. The would-be executioners of an accused adulteress encircled Jesus and the woman. Jesus said to them: "He who is without sin among you, let him be the first to throw a stone at her." (John 8:7)

What style did Jesus use to deal with this conflict? Can you think of other times when Jesus used this style? *(p. 72)*

*Answer: Loving confrontation.*

b. Read the following Proverb: "Better is open rebuke than hidden love. Wounds from a friend can be trusted." (Proverbs 27:5–6, NIV)

How can the "open rebuke" of "a friend" be helpful? *(p. 72)*

*Answer: Because it will help you deal with the truth and thus help heal a wound. If you operate according to the truth of God's Word and acknowledge your own weaknesses and failures, you will not leave yourself as open to Satan's lies.*

## CONSTRUCTION
(10–15 minutes)

> *This **Construction** project assists each couple in recognizing their usual method of dealing with conflicts.*

*Instruct each couple to answer the five questions together. As couples talk, announce when one minute is left.*

1. Think of a recent misunderstanding between you and your spouse. (It may have been over finances, children, vacation plans, choices, schedule, relatives, clothing, the car, etc.) How did you each respond? Circle your answer.

| HUSBAND | WIFE |
|---|---|
| Fight to Win | Fight to Win |
| Withdraw | Withdraw |
| Yield | Yield |
| Lovingly Confront | Lovingly Confront |

2. How did you feel when your mate used his/her approach to dealing with this conflict?

_____

_____

3. What would you do differently next time?

_____

_____

4. What would you prefer your mate to do differently next time?

_____

_____

## BLUEPRINTS (continued)
(20–35 minutes)

> This **Blueprints** section examines Jesus' method of dealing with conflicts and encourages couples to identify ways they may lovingly confront each other.

## C. Steps to Loving Confrontation

The words *loving* and *confrontation* don't appear to be complimentary. One word is "friendly" while the other tends to make you want to fight back. However, the combination of these two words into the phrase "loving confrontation" describes an important approach to resolving conflict. Loving confrontation is the balanced use of truth and love.

1. STEP ONE: Look inward.

Read Galatians 6:1:

> Brethren, even if a man is caught in any trespass, you who are spiritual, restore such a one in a spirit of gentleness; looking to yourselves, lest you too be tempted.

a. According to this passage, what three prerequisites should you meet before you correct someone? *(p. 74)*

*Answer: We need to be spiritual, we need to have a spirit of gentleness, and we need to "look to ourselves" to make sure we aren't tempted in the same way.*

b. Why is looking inward before confrontation so important? *(p. 74)*

*Answer: If we do not look inward, we may approach the confrontation with the wrong spirit—of pride, rather than gentleness and love. Also, we need to make sure we are not guilty of the same problem we are confronting the person about!*

2. STEP TWO: Pick the right time and place.

Read Proverbs 25:11: "Like apples of gold in settings of silver is a word spoken in right circumstances."

a. How would you define the "right circumstances" for loving confrontation in your marriage? *(p. 75)*

*Tip: You could have couples give their answers to each other, telling one another what words, actions and/or attitudes would convey love at a time of confrontation. After several minutes, comment that hearing how others answered that question can help people become more aware of ways to communicate love in these difficult moments. Invite volunteers to share their responses.*

b. MEN: What are the typically appropriate and inappropriate times or settings for your wife to bring up a difficult but necessary issue with you? *(p. 75)*

c. WOMEN: What are the typically appropriate and inappropriate times or settings for your husband to bring up a difficult but necessary issue with you? *(p. 75)*

*Tip: After several minutes, request that several men share times or settings when it is inappropriate to be confronted by their wives. Ask several women to share inappropriate times or settings for being confronted by their husbands. Repeat the process, asking both groups some of the appropriate times they wrote down.*

3. STEP THREE: Speak the truth in love.

Read the following directive from Ephesians 4:15:

> Speaking the truth in love, we are to grow up in all aspects into Him, who is the head, even Christ.

*Tip: Choose someone who hasn't spoken yet to read.*

a. What does it mean to speak the truth in love? *(p. 75)*

*Answer: It means that the truth as you see it should be presented gently, regarding your mate's needs as more important than your own.*

b. How have you applied this principle in your marriage? *(p. 76)*

c. What happens to a relationship when one person speaks truthfully, but without love? *(p. 76)*

   ***Answer:*** *The truth can bruise a person if it is told harshly or used as a weapon.*

d. What happens to a relationship where there is love without truth? *(p. 76)*

   ***Answer:*** *Confrontation and correction never occur, because one mate is too afraid of hurting the other with the truth. The person who needs to hear the truth is robbed of a chance to grow, and small issues can grow into large ones because they are never resolved.*

e. Which is easier for you to share, love or truth? Why? *(p. 76)*

*Read* **HomeBuilders Principle #7: For confrontation to benefit a relationship, truth must be shared with love.**

f. Even if you choose the right time and setting, you still need to approach the subject with proper focus. Fill in the following blanks, which pinpoint the proper focus for loving confrontation *(p. 77)*:

| INSTEAD OF FOCUSING ON: | FOCUS ON: |
| --- | --- |
| many issues | *one issue* |
| the person | *the problem* |
| character | *behavior* |
| generalizations | *specifics* |
| judgment of actions | *expression of feelings* |
| past grievances | *current situation* |
| judgment of motives | *observation of facts* |
| who's winning or losing | *mutual understanding* |

## D. The Wrong Way to Confront: A Case Study

*Tip: Instruct everyone to silently read the confrontation printed in the study guide, marking a check by each statement they think is a mistake in attempting "loving confrontation."*

### CASE STUDY

"Honey, it seems that every time you are with my relatives you get real quiet. What is it . . . don't you like them? Maybe it's my brother . . . or Mom. . . . You won't even look her in the eye when she talks to you. What's wrong with you? Look at these family pictures at Christmas. I think you are actually refusing to smile. How long has it been since you called my dad and suggested having breakfast with him? You know he'd love it. Why are you doing this?"

1. What mistakes do you see in this attempt at "loving confrontation"? *(p.77)*

*Answer: Mistakes include the following: Several statements are judgments of the other person's actions or motives; the focus is definitely on the person, not really on the problem; too many different issues are raised at the same time.*

*Tip: Invite volunteers to share the mistakes they marked, telling why they feel each was handled inappropriately. Be prepared to point out additional possibilities.*

2. What's a better way to handle this confrontation? *(p.77)*

*Tip: Prompt group members to be specific in telling what they would say or do to deal better with the areas of concern.*

## E. Reflection

What one point or idea was most helpful to you in this session? Why? *(p.78)*

## MAKE A DATE

> Each **HomeBuilders Project** is essential for couples to do to-
> gether during the week. This week's interaction will help couples
> improve their skills in using "I" messages and identify ways in
> which to improve their focus in lovingly confronting one another.

Ask each couple to look at the **Make a Date** section of the study guide,
then agree on a time this week to complete **HomeBuilders Project #3** together.

Remind the group that at the next session you will ask each couple to share
one thing they discovered or discussed during their **HomeBuilders Project.**
Point out that there is an optional project this week for those who wish to
apply what they learned in this session more directly. Also, remind group
members to bring their calendars to the next session as an aid in scheduling their next date with their mates.

## RECOMMENDED READING

> Encourage couples to locate this book and to read all or part of
> it before the next session.

**Caring Enough to Confront,** by David Augsburger.
    Discussing trust, anger, change, prejudice, blame, guilt, loyalty, and con-
science, the author describes a lifestyle for Christians who care enough to
risk confronting others when differences become important. An excellent
book for Christians who care about relationships—adults, youth, pastors,
couples.

Dismiss in prayer, or invite couples to pray together.

Invite everyone to enjoy a time of fellowship and refreshments.

## HOMEBUILDERS PROJECT #4a

### Individually: 30 minutes

1. Review the three "Steps to Loving Confrontation" in the **Blueprints** section.

2. In which of these three areas do you personally struggle the most?

_____

_____

_____

_____

### Interact As a Couple: 30 minutes

1. Go over your answers to the question you answered individually.

2. Come to a consensus on the best way to handle confrontation in your marriage.

3. One of the biggest mistakes couples make in confrontation is adopting a "you" focus in their confrontations. "You" messages usually come across as attacks or criticisms. They seek to fix blame on the other person. "I" messages are usually much clearer and more honest, and they don't place blame.

   Using "I" instead of "you" statements is much less threatening to the person you're confronting. The following exercise will give you practice in recognizing and using "I" language and other ways of focusing confrontation appropriately.

Work together to turn the "you" messages in the following chart into "I" messages. To give you an example, the first two are done for you.

| "YOU" MESSAGES | "I" MESSAGES |
|---|---|
| You don't understand me! | I feel misunderstood! |
| You don't budget our money! | I'm concerned about our finances. Can you help me? |
| You are gone too much! | _____ |
| You are always late! | _____ |
| You are blaming everything on me! | _____ |
| You make me angry! | _____ |
| You never tell me you love me! | _____ |
| (Write a few that you tend to use:) | _____ |
| _____ | _____ |
| _____ | _____ |
| _____ | _____ |

4. As pointed out in the session, loving confrontation often is misfocused. Check the areas in which you most often get out of focus as you confront your spouse:

_____ Raising many issues at once instead of just one issue at a time.

_____ Focusing on the person rather than the problem.

_____ Focusing on my mate's character rather than specific behavior.

_____ Using generalizations rather than specifics.

_____          Judging actions rather than expressing feelings.

_____          Using "You" statements rather than "I" statements.

_____          Judging motives rather than observing facts.

_____          Concentrating on who is winning or losing rather than striving for mutual understanding.

5. Pray together, asking the Lord for His help and wisdom as you deal with conflicts.

Remember to bring your calendar for **Make a Date** to your next session.

## HOMEBUILDERS PROJECT #4b (Optional)

### Individually: 30 minutes

1. Write down one concern about which you feel you need to confront your mate.

2. Using the information discussed in the **Blueprints** section and in **HomeBuilders Project #4a,** write out how you will confront your mate on this subject.

3. Review again the information from Session Three on developing proper listening habits.

### Interact As a Couple: 30–60 minutes

1. Take turns sharing your concerns with each other. As your mate confronts you, be sure to apply proper listening habits as you seek mutual understanding of the problem.

2. Spend some time in prayer together, asking for His strength to work through you.

Remember to bring your calendar for **Make a Date** to your next session.

## SESSION FIVE
*Forgiving*

## FOCUS

For peace to replace conflict,
both husband and wife
must take responsibility to
forgive each other.

### Objectives

In this session, you will help each couple comprehend the impact on their marriage of asking for and receiving forgiveness as you guide them to:

■ Recognize ways in which God's forgiveness is a model for their forgiveness;

■ Clarify the difference between actions based on faith and those based on feelings;

■ Identify practical steps for both requesting and granting forgiveness and learn how these steps can be implemented in their marriage.

### Overall Comments

Session Five focuses on another critical aspect of dealing with conflict. This session highlights a common obstacle to conflict resolution in marriage—an unwillingness to ask for, grant, or receive forgiveness. Our extended families and circles of friends probably all include one or more examples of a relationship gone sour because of a lack of forgiveness. Couples today need to know practical, daily steps for reconciliation. Only within a relationship with God are we able to find the Source of forgiveness.

## WARM UP
(15–20 minutes)

---

> The **Warm Up** *focuses attention on the topic of forgiveness by considering a couple who find themselves unable to forgive.*

---

*Greet people as they arrive. Share personal expressions of appreciation for people's participation and support in earlier sessions. Tell people of your appreciation for the opportunity to get to know them better.*

*Start the session on time.*

1. Share something you learned from **HomeBuilders Project #4.** *(p. 86)*

   ***Tip:*** *Ask for a show of hands of the couples who kept their date with each other to complete **HomeBuilders Project #4.** Invite volunteers to share an insight gained from their **HomeBuilders Project.***

2. Read the following case study *(p. 86)*:

   ### CASE STUDY

   Charlie and Ellen have come to you for counsel. They are Christians, but during your time together they express intense feelings of anger and bitterness toward one another. You know well that there must be a history of selfishness, disappointment, and mistrust between them. You are relieved to hear of their faithfulness to each other but wonder how such resentment has grown over these twelve years of marriage.

   "I can never feel any forgiveness toward Charlie anymore," Ellen says, while Charlie retorts, "I'd like to forgive my wife, but I can't change the way I feel. I can't change the past."

   a. What do you think might have contributed to this couple's coldness toward each other over the years? *(p. 86)*

*Tip: This is a good place to have group members think back over the previous four sessions and draw from them possible reasons for this couple's ongoing conflict (problems with recognizing conflict, reluctance to be transparent, poor listening, and difficulties in confronting lovingly).*

b. What do you think their relationship will be like in another five years? *(p. 87)*

_____

_____

c. How would you counsel them? *(p. 87)*

_____

_____

## BLUEPRINTS
(25–35 minutes)

*This **Blueprints** section presents God's plan for forgiveness and will help couples see that forgiving the other person is the only reasonable response to experiencing forgiveness from God.*

### A. What Is Forgiveness?

1. Think back to a time in your life when you received forgiveness from another person for something you did to him or her.

a. Describe the situation. *(p. 88)*

_____

_____

b. How did you feel before and after you received forgiveness? *(p. 88)*

_____

_____

2. From that experience, what would you say it means to forgive another person? What is forgiveness? *(p. 88)*

3. Our Lord provides the best model for what forgiveness is. What do each of the following passages say about God's forgiveness? *(p. 89)*

*Tip: Call on a different group member to read each of the passages. Then lead the group in responding to the question, "What do these passages say about God's forgiveness?" It is vital for each group member to recognize the breadth of God's forgiveness in Christ. Instruct them to look for words in these passages that define the extent of God's forgiveness.*

God was in Christ reconciling the world to Himself, not counting their trespasses against them. (2 Corinthians 5:19)

*Answer: God took the initiative; He doesn't count our transgressions.*

There is therefore now no condemnation for those who are in Christ Jesus. (Romans 8:1)

*Answer: Once we have received Christ, there is no condemnation against us.*

And their sins and their lawless deeds I will remember no more. (Hebrews 10:17)

*Answer: God completely forgets our sins once they are forgiven.*

He made you alive together with Him, having forgiven us all our transgressions. (Colossians 2:13)

*Answer: He gave us life; all our transgressions are forgiven.*

Since hurt and disappointment and unmet expectations are inevitable in a marriage relationship, we need to know how to respond when we experience them. Some people don't want to admit their hurt; they withdraw and hide their feelings. Others want to get even by inflicting the same type of hurt. But just as God forgave us of every sin we ever committed against Him, so do we need to forgive our mates. By forgiving your mate, you give up the right to punish him or her. And you decide, as an act of your will, to not hold your mate's mistakes against him or her.

4. Why is the kind of forgiveness described in the previous verses and statement so essential in a marriage relationship? *(p. 90)*

   *Answer: Without it, neither of you will be set free from your conflict and your bitterness.*

5. Why do you at times find it difficult to ask your mate for forgiveness? *(p. 90)*

   _____

   _____

6. Why do you find it difficult to grant forgiveness when you've been wronged? *(p. 90)*

   _____

   _____

*Read aloud* **HomeBuilders Principle #8: You must forgive your mate as God has forgiven you.**

## B. How to Ask for Forgiveness

Read the following passage, the well-known story of the prodigal son:

> A certain man had two sons; and the younger of them said to his father, "Father, give me the share of the estate that falls to me." And he divided his wealth between them. And not many days later, the younger son gathered everything together and went on a journey into a distant country, and there he squandered his estate with loose living.
>
> Now when he had spent everything, a severe famine occurred in that country, and he began to be in need. And he went and attached

himself to one of the citizens of that country, and he sent him into his fields to feed swine. And he was longing to fill his stomach with the pods that the swine were eating, and no one was giving anything to him. But when he came to his senses, he said, "How many of my father's hired men have more than enough bread, but I am dying here with hunger! I will get up and go to my father, and will say to him, 'Father, I have sinned against heaven, and in your sight; I am no longer worthy to be called your son; make me as one of your hired men.'"

And he got up and came to his father. But while he was still a long way off, his father saw him, and felt compassion for him, and ran and embraced him, and kissed him. And the son said to him, "Father, I have sinned against heaven and in your sight; I am no longer worthy to be called your son."

But the father said to his slaves, "Quickly bring out the best robe and put it on him, and put a ring on his hand and sandals on his feet; and bring the fattened calf, kill it, and let us eat and be merry; for this son of mine was dead, and has come to life again; he was lost, and has been found." (Luke 15:11–24)

This passage illustrates three steps to asking for forgiveness:

1. STEP ONE: Take responsibility for your wrong actions.

   a. What indicates that the prodigal son took responsibility? *(p. 91)*

   *Answer: He returned home, and he was willing to pay off his debt as a hired man.*

   b. Why is taking responsibility an essential part of asking and receiving forgiveness? *(p. 91)*

   *Answer: Taking responsibility requires humility, a willingness to admit fault, and a willingness to take action.*

2. STEP TWO: State your error and humbly ask the person to forgive you.

   How did the prodigal son accomplish this step? *(p. 92)*

*Answer: He returned home in complete humility, admitting he had sinned in God's sight and in his father's sight. Note: He didn't specifically say, "Father, will you forgive me?", but the story still represents the steps a person should take to restore a relationship.*

3. STEP THREE: Take steps to change your behavior and/or make restitution.

   a. How did the prodigal son accomplish this step? *(p. 92)*

   *Answer: He was willing to be one of his father's "hired men."*

   b. When a person doesn't try to change the behavior he or she asked forgiveness for, what does this do to the relationship? *(p. 92)*

   *Answer: It cheapens the forgiveness, and it can harden the heart of the person who granted the forgiveness. Note: If someone in your group brings up the fact that some people may be reluctant to ask forgiveness for a certain offense because he or she feels unable to change the behavior, mention that the main point is being willing to try. Also, the Holy Spirit can provide supernatural power to change behavior when the Christian doesn't feel able to do it.*

   c. Share an example of someone who asked for and received your forgiveness for an offense, but never changed his or her behavior. What did this do to the relationship? *(p. 92)*

   _____

   _____

   d. Share an example—from your marriage, if possible—where you or your mate did change your behavior after receiving forgiveness. *(p. 92)*

   _____

   _____

## C. How to Grant Forgiveness

Read the following passage:

> This I say therefore . . . that you walk no longer just as the Gentiles also walk, in the futility of their mind. . . . Lay aside the old self . . . be renewed in the spirit of your mind . . . and put on the new self, which in the likeness of God has been created in righteousness and holiness of the truth. . . . Let all bitterness and wrath and anger and clamor and slander be put away from you, along with all malice. And be kind to one another, tender-hearted, *forgiving* each other, just as God in Christ also has forgiven you. (Ephesians 4:17, 22–24, 31–32, emphasis added)

1. STEP ONE: Give up the right to punish your mate.

   a. What does Ephesians 4:31 tell us to do with our negative feelings? *(p. 93)*

   *Answer: God commands us to forgive each other because He knows that it will likely not happen out of an overwhelming feeling of mercy.*

2. STEP TWO: Yield to God's command to forgive, in the power of the Holy Spirit.

   a. Read the following passages:

   > But the fruit of the Spirit is love, joy, peace, patience, kindness, goodness, faithfulness, gentleness, self-control; against such things there is no law. (Galatians 5:22–23)

   > And do not get drunk with wine, for that is dissipation, but be filled with the Spirit. (Ephesians 5:18)

   Why is it important to be filled with the Holy Spirit as you seek to forgive your mate? *(p. 93)*

   *Answer: The Holy Spirit provides the power to do something which you may feel unable to do.*

*Read aloud* **HomeBuilders Principle #9: The power of forgiveness lies in God's Spirit as He is given control in your heart.**

b. Why do you think God co*mmands* us to forgive rather than asking us to forgive when we feel like it? *(p. 94)*

*Answer: He doesn't want to make it an option, and He wants us to rely on Him.*

c. Think of a time when you obeyed God even though you didn't feel like it. How did God bless you as a result? *(p. 94)*

_____

_____

*Tip: Prime the group's memories with a brief story of your own. Look into your past, recalling difficult in-law relationships, co-worker communications, sibling rivalry, stressful times in your marriage, etc. Dig up a time when you were obedient to God in treating them properly and He blessed you as a result.*

3. STEP THREE: Don't dwell on the past.

a. How does the Lord regard our past sins for which He has forgiven us? *(p. 94)*

*Answer: He forgets them.*

b. Read Isaiah 43:18–19:

Do not call to mind the former things, or ponder things of the past. Behold, I will do something new, now it will spring forth; will you not be aware of it? I will even make a roadway in the wilderness, rivers in the desert.

How can you apply this passage to the subject of forgiveness? *(p. 94)*

_____

_____

c. When you choose to forgive your mate in light of God's forgiveness and in obedience to Him, what kind of freedom will you likely experience? *(p. 95)*

*Answer: Forgiving someone can help set you free from bitterness and negative thoughts. You'll be able to show love and experience love in return, and this will increase oneness in your marriage.*

*Read aloud the quote from Dr. Lewis Smedes:*

To forgive is to set a prisoner free . . . and discover that the prisoner was you.

Dr. Lewis Smedes

*Read aloud* **HomeBuilders Principle #10: Forgiving your mate sets you free to experience love and oneness.**

## CONSTRUCTION
(10–15 minutes)

*This **Construction** project encourages couples to examine and improve patterns of forgiveness in their marriage. Instruct each couple to answer the two questions individually, then to share their responses with each other. As couples talk, announce when one minute is left.*

### CASE STUDY (continued)

Charlie and Ellen are still with you, trading verbal cannonballs.

ELLEN: "Charlie makes me feel so unlovable. He always has to be right. The things he has said to me when angered, the way he treats me around the kids, his arrogant ways in front of my parents . . . I just can't let him get by with this. Why should I forgive him? He made his bed, let him sleep in it!"

CHARLIE: "If I've hurt her, then she deserves it. I work hard all day to provide for her needs, and all I hear is griping. I can never do enough, never say things just right; I can never be kind enough to her folks. She's done more than her share to make me miserable. I've only balanced the scales!"

1. What do Charlie and Ellen need to do along with choosing to forgive each other? *(p. 96)*

_____

_____

2. How should you apply the phrase, "just as God in Christ also has forgiven you," when:

   a. You find yourself continuing to think about things your mate has done to you in the past? *(p. 96)*

_____

_____

   b. You want to remind your mate of a way he or she has hurt you in the past? *(p. 97)*

_____

_____

## MAKE A DATE

*HomeBuilders Project #5 will help couples personally understand more of God's forgiveness. Also, there will be an opportunity for them to deal with the need to offer forgiveness to each other. The time they spend talking together may well be a large step in the direction of ongoing forgiveness for years to come.*

Ask each couple to look at the **Make a Date** section of the study guide, then agree on a time this week to complete **HomeBuilders Project #5**.

*Remind the group that at the next session you will ask each couple to share one thing they discovered or discussed during their **HomeBuilders Project.***

## RECOMMENDED READING

> *Encourage couples to locate the books listed in their study guides.*

**Caring Enough to Forgive,** by David Augsburger.

David Augsburger is a forceful writer with a compassionate heart for the needs of people. This book is the second in a new series of "Caring Enough" books.

**How Can It Be All Right When Everything Is All Wrong?,** by Lewis B. Smedes.

The experience of "real believing" is the subject of this remarkable book. Author Lewis Smedes shows what it means—and how it feels—to get in touch with "the kind of believing you do with your deepest self, down deep where your primeval feelings flow." *How Can It Be All Right When Everything Is All Wrong?* helps us to grow in awareness of the presence of God inside us. This book doesn't explain away the fact that things get bad. Instead, it helps us move beyond a disheartening present by being open to God and the certainty that things are fundamentally all right.

**How to Experience God's Love and Forgiveness,** by Bill Bright.

This booklet is one of ten that give you the "how-to's" of consistent Christian living. All ten are excellent for personal enrichment and as gifts for growing Christians.

**Love Life for Every Married Couple,** by Ed Wheat.

In this book, Dr. Wheat explores marital conflict in a straightforward manner, focusing on the reasons why couples experience frustration and unhappiness in their love life.

*Dismiss in prayer, or invite individuals to offer brief prayers expressing thanks for their mate and for the opportunity to grow in the marriage relationship.*

*Invite everyone to enjoy a time of fellowship and refreshments.*

## HOMEBUILDERS PROJECT #5

**Individually: 30 minutes**

1. Review the session in its entirety.

2. Complete the following two statements, to be shared with your mate:

    a. "My greatest difficulty in offering you forgiveness is _____
    _____."

    b. "The one thing that would make it easier for me to ask your forgive-
    ness is _____."

3. Write down some instances in which you have received forgiveness from your wife/husband and have seen healing occur in your relationship as a result.

_____

_____

_____

4. What are some things for which you need to ask your wife's/husband's forgiveness now?

_____

**Interact As a Couple: 30–40 minutes**

1. Share your answers to the first three questions you answered individually (questions 1–3).

2. HUSBAND: Ask your wife what you can do to make it easier for her to admit wrong and seek your forgiveness. Record her input below:

_____

_____

_____

3. WIFE: Ask your husband what you can do to make it easier for him to admit wrong and seek your forgiveness. Record his input below:

_____

_____

_____

4. Now it's time to practice what you've been learning. Share your answers to the fourth question you answered individually (question 4).

5. Pray together. Thank God for His unending grace and for His Holy Spirit, who enables you to forgive each other "just as God in Christ has forgiven you."

Remember to bring your calendar for **Make a Date** to your next session.

## SESSION SIX
*A Blessing for an Insult*

### FOCUS

People have a natural
tendency to respond to hurts with anger.
God promises to help us
exchange these natural reactions
for supernatural responses.

### Objectives

In this final session, you will help each couple respond to insults within
their marriage in an active and reactive sense as you guide them to:

■ Identify the active and reactive responses available to a couple;

■ Contrast the natural tendency to retaliate by insult with the supernatural ability to respond with a blessing; and

■ Contemplate the example of Jesus in responding with a blessing.

### Overall Comments

Session Six is perhaps the most practical of these six sessions. Life is lived
in the insult arena, whether it be subtle barrages or out-and-out verbal war.

Most people can sit down and calmly assess what should be done when a
conflict arises. You may have been impressed by the quality of insight shared
by group members in previous sessions as they analyzed the case studies
and discussed their own intentions. When caught in the midst of marital
battle, however, most people tend to react immediately and instinctively,
and all those fine principles seemingly go out the window. Far too many
conflicts escalate to volatile levels, not because the original problem was so

97

crucial, but because things were said or done in haste and anger, making matters even more difficult to resolve.

This session deals directly with our innate tendency to strike back when offended, showing how God offers a much better alternative: a blessing instead of an insult.

### WARM UP
(15–20 minutes)

*Greet people as they arrive. Comment to a few couples that time has flown and that you are already down to the last session. Begin now to plant anticipation for another study sometime in the future.*

*As always, make a point of starting the session on time.*

1. Begin this session by sharing one thing you learned from **HomeBuilders Project #5.** *(p. 104)*

2. In the following situations, what would be the normal, natural response? *(p. 104)*

   *Tip: Encourage people to act as if they were actually talking with their mates in each situation.*

   SITUATION A: Your husband has just embarrassed you at a party by disclosing personal information.

   SITUATION B: Your wife is quietly watching television. You slip up behind her in a romantic mood and begin rubbing her neck. She snaps, "Don't you see I'm involved in this program?"

3. What do you think would be the best thing to say to your mate in each situation? *(pp. 104–105)*

***Possible Answers, Situation A:*** *"I appreciate it when you talk more deeply than just football and hunting, honey. However, I feel that our conversation with the Lewises tonight may have been touching on things that should be discussed only between the two of us. How do you feel about it?"*

***Possible Answers, Situation B:*** *"Oops, I'm sorry, honey! When there is a break, let me know if you would like some popcorn to go along with the show, okay?"*

## BLUEPRINTS
### (20–25 minutes)

> *This **Blueprints** section talks of resolving conflict in an active way. We will look at the nature of real love and evaluate the results of acting accordingly in a relationship.*

## A. Disappointment and Hurt Are Inevitable in Marriage

1. Why is it that the best of friends can sometimes end up bitter enemies? *(p. 106)*

**Answer:** *When you trust and love someone—as a friend or as a spouse— you feel the pain more acutely when that person does something that hurts you. Sometimes best friends allow bitterness to grow in their hearts, and they are too proud to take steps to reconcile with each other. Then they try to hurt the other person just as they have been hurt.*

2. Why are hurt and disappointment inevitable in marriage? *(p. 106)*

**Answer:** *First, we are sinful human beings. Second, people's expectations generally don't come close to what reality is; therefore, when their expectations aren't met, they experience negative feelings such as hurt and disappointment.*

Since hurt and disappointment will occur in your marriage, you need to decide how you want to respond to these painful experiences. You have a choice: you can return an insult with another insult, or you can give a blessing instead.

## B. Returning an Insult with an Insult

Read the following scriptural command:

> To sum up, let all be harmonious, sympathetic, brotherly, kind-hearted, and humble in spirit; not returning evil for evil, or insult for insult, but giving a blessing instead; for you were called for the very purpose that you might inherit a blessing. For "let him who means to love life and see good days refrain his tongue from evil and his lips from speaking guile. And let him . . . seek peace and pursue it. For the eyes of the Lord are upon the righteous, and His ears attend to their prayer, but the face of the Lord is against those who do evil." (1 Peter 3:8–12)

1. What does "returning evil for evil, or insult for insult" mean? *(p. 107)*

   ***Answer:*** *Someone insults you, so you insult him or her back. Returning evil for evil causes people in a relationship to grow farther and farther apart.*

   The insult-for-insult relationship is defined as "meaning to hurt by remark or action." A person is hurt, so he wants to get even, saying in essence, "What you did hurt me, so I am going to hurt you back." This type of relationship is rooted in an unforgiving and hardened heart attitude. Selfishness is at its core.

2. How do you see children "returning evil for evil, or insult for insult" as they relate to each other? *(p. 107)*

   ***Possible Answers:*** *"So, you're not so smart yourself!". . . "Takes one to know one!"*

   ***Tip:*** *Encourage your group to recall several typical childhood reactions to insults or to share some things they've heard their children say. These are funny to rehearse.*

3. How have you seen this type of response in your own marriage or in others' marriages? *(p. 107)*

*Tip: Be prepared to illustrate from your own marriage or from ones that you have observed. (Be careful that you do not imply that the example was from any of the marriages gathered in your group.)*

4. What situations or circumstances tend to provoke this type of response in you? *(p. 107)*

5. What happens to a marriage if it never grows out of the "insult for insult" mode? How have you seen couples unleash the "insult for insult" response on each other during divorce proceedings? *(p. 108)*

*Tip: Be ready with your own examples to "prime the pump" if necessary.*

## C. The Power of the "Blessing for Insult" Relationship

1. Read 1 Peter 3:8–12 again. What does "giving a blessing" mean? *(p. 108)*

*Answer: Returning an act of kindness (rather than another insult) for an insult.*

2. What additional insights do you gain about giving a blessing from the following verses? *(p. 108)*

> Never pay back evil for evil to anyone. Respect what is right in the sight of all men. (Romans 12:17)

*Answer: We're commanded to not insult a person who insults us, but to seek after what is good for him or her.*

> But I say to you who hear, love your enemies, do good to those who hate you, bless those who curse you, pray for those who mistreat you. (Luke 6:27–28)

*Answer: We are actively to "love" and "do good" to people who do evil to us.*

The blessing-for-insult relationship can be defined as "continual, active kindness." It is rooted in a forgiving and gracious heart. It means that when your mate disappoints you or hurts you, your responsibility is to find a way to bless him or her. Giving a blessing means that your hope is in God and His Word and that you choose to do good to another regardless of what he or she has done to you.

*Tip: The following chart contains important information, but it's not essential for the discussion. If you are short on time, just summarize the chart briefly and encourage people to read it on their own later.*

| INSULT-FOR-INSULT RELATIONSHIP | BLESSING-FOR-INSULT RELATIONSHIP |
|---|---|
| Human perspective | Divine perspective |
| Based on selfishness and circumstances | Based on God's Word, the unseen |
| Results: punishment, anger and barriers | Results: purposeful action, transparency |
| Reactive: emotionally centered; following natural instincts | Responsive: God-centered supernatural response |
| Attitude: tear down, depreciate, provoke the other person more | Attitude: build up, appreciate; provokes confession, godliness, and blessing |

*Read aloud* **HomeBuilders Principle #11: Returning a blessing for an insult helps defeat the cycle of selfishness which can corrode a marriage relationship.**

3. What are some things you've seen your mate do to give a blessing after an insult? *(p. 109)*

_____

_____

4. What are some other practical ways you can give a blessing? *(p. 109)*

---

---

## D. Three Steps to a "Blessing" Relationship

First Peter 3:8–12 outlines three simple steps leading to blessing relationships.

1. STEP ONE: "refrain your . . . tongue from evil"

   Why do you think it is so important to control your tongue? *(p. 110)*

   **Answer:** *Most insults are verbal. If you can control your tongue, you'll probably eliminate most of your insults.*

2. STEP TWO: "turn away from evil and do good"

   How do you "turn away from evil"? What kind of impact does this response have on a conflict? *(p. 110)*

   **Answer:** *Before acting, force yourself to think through your alternatives. You have to choose deliberately not to respond to an insult with actions that have any kind of evil motives.*

3. STEP THREE: "seek peace and pursue it."

   What is one way you can apply this step in your marriage? *(p. 110)*

---

---

## CONSTRUCTION
### (10–15 minutes)

> *This **Construction** Project gives couples time to think of blessings they can give to one another.*

**Individually:**

Conflict often grows out of differences in the things we like to do. For example, the husband wants to spend his Saturday afternoon watching college football on television, but his wife wants him to catch up on yard work. Or the wife likes the window open in the bedroom at night, while her husband wants it shut.

Sometimes giving a blessing means regarding others as more important than yourself. Read the following passage:

> Do nothing from selfishness or empty conceit, but with humility of mind let each of you regard one another as more important than himself; do not merely look out for your own personal interests, but also for the interests of others. Have this attitude in yourselves which was also in Christ Jesus, who, although He existed in the form of God, did not regard equality with God a thing to be grasped, but emptied Himself, taking the form of a bond-servant, and being made in the likeness of men. And being found in appearance as a man, He humbled Himself by becoming obedient to the point of death, even death on a cross. (Philippians 2:3–8)

What are some examples of how you could give a blessing by doing what your mate wants instead of what you want?

_____

_____

### Interact As a Couple:

Share your answers with each other.

## BLUEPRINTS (Continued)

### E. The Hope of the Holy Spirit.

1. Why is giving a blessing after an insult so difficult? *(p. 113)*

   ***Answer:*** *Our natural inclination often is to strike back. We want revenge.*

2. Read 1 Peter 2:20–24:

   > For what credit is there if, when you sin and are harshly treated, you endure it with patience? But if when you do what is right and suffer for it you patiently endure it, this finds favor with God. For

you have been called for this purpose, since Christ also suffered for you, leaving you an example for you to follow in His steps, who committed no sin, nor was any deceit found in His mouth; and while being reviled, He did not revile in return; while suffering, He uttered no threats, but kept entrusting Himself to Him who judges righteously.

*Tip: Have the entire group read this passage together in unison.*

a. How did Christ respond to insult? *(p. 113)*

**Answer:** *He entrusted Himself to the One who judges righteously.*

b. What does it mean to entrust yourself "to Him who judges righteously"? Why is this important when working through conflict? *(p. 113)*

**Answer:** *"Vengeance is mine . . . says the Lord" (Romans 12:19)! Entrusting to Him means letting Him decide—since that is for Him to do—if the person or the incident needs further judgment or punishment. In conflict, we tend to want to pronounce judgment and get even.*

c. Can you recall a time when, after an insult, you entrusted yourself to the Father and, in the power of the Holy Spirit, experienced the supernatural ability to respond with a blessing? Share a few of the details. *(p. 114)*

---

*Tip: This is a very important part of this session because it is a time for hope. The group needs to know that God has shown us how to deal with insult through the model of His Son and has given us the power, through His Holy Spirit, to live above an insulting reaction. The practical experiences discussed here will bring great hope to your group. Make sure that you and your spouse have thought deeply about this question and are ready to offer your own experiences.*

*ead aloud **HomeBuilders Principle #12: As you depend on the Holy pirit for wisdom and power, you will develop the forgiving and graious heart you need to respond with a blessing rather than an insult.***

## F. Conclusion

*Tip: This final section provides you the opportunity to wrap up the entire six-session study. Encourage couples to think back over all they've learned and to pinpoint some principles they need to concentrate on applying in their marriage.*

1. How have the principles you've learned in this entire study helped you begin to resolve conflict in your marriage? *(p. 114)*

_____

_____

2. What are some principles you feel you need to practice or emphasize more in the future? *(p. 114)*

_____

_____

## MAKE A DATE

> *This week's project will help couples move beyond instinctive insult reactions and begin to nurture responses of blessing. There will be time to express value seen in the other person, confess tendencies to react with insult, and to talk together about what it means to "entrust" to the Father.*

*Ask each couple to look at the **Make a Date** section of the study guide, then agree on a time this week to complete **HomeBuilders Project #6***

## RECOMMENDED READING

> *Encourage couples to make a habit of reading helpful material about marriage regularly.*

**Lonely Husbands, Lonely Wives,** by Dennis Rainey. "Married but lonely" would describe the condition of many people today. Conflicting work schedules, differences in upbringing and expectations, selfishness, unexpected difficulties, and countless other factors conspire to isolate marriage partners from each other. This tendency will continue, says Dennis Rainey, unless the couple has a plan of action to combat these destructive forces and deliberately works to build oneness and intimacy. Here is a master plan for oneness, based squarely on biblical principles, to enable you to build a marriage of strength and lasting intimacy.

**Building Your Mate's Self-Esteem,** by Dennis and Barbara Rainey. In this book, Dennis and Barbara Rainey offer you insight into God's selfless, self-giving formula for marriage. This intensely practical book teaches you how to deal with the haunting problems of the past, how to give your mate the freedom to fail, how to help your mate be liberated from self-doubt, and provides other creative ideas to help you achieve immediate results.

**The Blessing,** by Gary Smalley and John Trent. *The Blessing* is a common-sense depiction of a tradition that was old in the days of Isaac and Abraham, one that is pivotal to the understanding of a host of biblical truths. Gary Smalley and John Trent detail the five elements of the blessing: (1) meaningful touch, (2) the spoken word, (3) the expression of high value, (4) the description of a special future, and (5) the application of genuine commitment. This book offers solid, practical advice for individuals, families, counselors, and pastors.

*Dismiss in prayer.*

*Join hands with everyone in the group and conclude with a time of group praise for what God has taught you and for the good experiences ahead in each marriage.*

## HOMEBUILDERS PROJECT #6

**Individually: 30 minutes**

1. Review the entire **Blueprints** section.

2. People typically react to an insult in one of two ways: withdrawing or attacking.

How would you rate your own tendency toward withdrawing or attacking in response to conflict? (Circle the appropriate number.)

WITHDRAW

| 1 | 2 | 3 | 4 | 5 | 6 | 7 | 8 | 9 | 10 |
|---|---|---|---|---|---|---|---|---|---|
| low | | | | | | | | | high |

ATTACK

| 1 | 2 | 3 | 4 | 5 | 6 | 7 | 8 | 9 | 10 |
|---|---|---|---|---|---|---|---|---|---|
| low | | | | | | | | | high |

3. How would you rate your mate's tendencies?

WITHDRAW

| 1 | 2 | 3 | 4 | 5 | 6 | 7 | 8 | 9 | 10 |
|---|---|---|---|---|---|---|---|---|---|
| low | | | | | | | | | high |

ATTACK

| 1 | 2 | 3 | 4 | 5 | 6 | 7 | 8 | 9 | 10 |
|---|---|---|---|---|---|---|---|---|---|
| low | | | | | | | | | high |

4. Use the chart on the following page to become a better student of yourself and your reactions. This exercise will also help you come up with the right responses to insulting remarks.

   a. Consider, "In what areas do I tend to react against my mate?" List the situations in the first column of the chart.

   b. List your typical responses to each situation in the second column.

   c. Rank the magnitude of the problems caused by each situation as (H) high, (M) medium, or (L) low and list your ranking in the third column.

   d. In the fourth column, list how you think you *should respond* in the situation.

| a. SITUATION | b. USUAL RESPONSE | c. MAGNITUDE OF PROBLEM | d. BETTER RESPONSE |
|---|---|---|---|
| | | | |
| | | | |
| | | | |
| | | | |
| | | | |

5. How can you better "seek peace and pursue it" in your marriage relationship?

_____

_____

6. Write down some past examples of how you have reacted to an insult by returning another insult. How could you have returned a blessing in each situation?

_____

_____

**Interact As a Couple: 25–30 minutes**

1. Share each of your answers from the individual section with each other, and look at each other's charts. If necessary, you may need to practice the principles from Session Five and ask for forgiveness.

2. Talk together about what it means to "entrust" yourself to "the One who judges righteously." How will each of you know when the other is doing that?

_____

_____

3. Pray together, asking the Lord to give you wisdom as you seek a blessing-for-insult relationship. Thank Him for the blessings that you will inherit, according to His promise, as you live according to His design.

## CONCLUSION
*Where Do You Go from Here?*

As we learned in this study, couples need to know how to resolve conflict if they desire to build a solid marriage. Of the available options, either worldly or biblical, the biblical guidelines God has ordained for us to use are clearly best. Often, the truths which Scripture unveils are simple, basic, and clear. This does not necessarily mean, however, that they are easy to implement on a practical, day-to-day basis.

Building your marriage upon these truths may not be popular today, but it will have powerful results. You have probably already caught some special glimpses of that power through your investment of study, discussion, and application. If the truth within this couples study has at times shaken your marriage, it has done so only to strengthen it. We hope you have experienced a sense of strengthening.

But let's not stop here! If this HomeBuilders Couples Series study has helped you and your marriage, let's go on. And in going on, why not ask other couples to join you? By personally beginning another HomeBuilders study, you will not only add additional mortar to your own marriage; you will help strengthen other marriages as well. As Christians, we are not just trying to improve ourselves . . . we are trying to reach the world! This is our ultimate objective in The HomeBuilders Couples Series. Will you now help us help others?

**Will you join us in touching lives and changing families?**

The following are some practical ways you can make a difference in families today:

1. Gather a group of couples (four to seven) and lead them through the six sessions of the HomeBuilders study you just completed.

2. Commit to participate in other HomeBuilders studies such as *Building Your Marriage, Strengthening Your Mate's Self-Esteem, Building Teamwork in Marriage,* or *Mastering Your Money in Marriage.*

3. Begin weekly family nights—teaching your children about Christ, the Bible, and the Christian life.

4. Host an Evangelistic Dinner Party—invite your non-Christian friends to your home and as a couple share your faith in Christ and the forgiveness of His Gospel.

5. Share the Good News of Jesus Christ with neighborhood children.

6. If you have attended the Family Life Conference, why not assist your pastor in counseling pre-marrieds using the material you received?

7. Talk to your pastor about renting The HomeBuilders Film Series for your church. This is a six-part series on marriage which is currently available for church showings.

For more information on any of the ministry opportunities mentioned above, contact your local church, or write:

> Family Ministry
> P.O. Box 23840
> Little Rock, AR 72221-3840
> (501)223-8663

## APPENDIX A
*The Four Spiritual Laws\**

Just as there are physical laws that govern the physical universe, so are there spiritual laws which govern your relationship with God.

> **Law One:** *God loves you and offers a wonderful plan for your life.*

### God's Love

"For God so loved the world, that He gave His only begotten Son, that whoever believes in Him should not perish, but have eternal life" (John 3:16).

### God's Plan

(Christ speaking) "I came that they might have life, and might have it abundantly" (that it might be full and meaningful) (John 10:10).

Why is it that most people are not experiencing the abundant life? Because . . .

> **Law Two:** *Man is sinful and separated from God. Therefore, he cannot know and experience God's love and plan for his life.*

### Man Is Sinful

"For all have sinned and fall short of the glory of God" (Romans 3:23).

Man was created to have fellowship with God; but, because of his stubborn self-will, chose to go his own independent way, and fellowship with God was broken. This self-will, characterized by an attitude of active rebellion or passive indifference, is evidence of what the Bible calls sin.

---

\* Written by Bill Bright. Copyright © Campus Crusade for Christ, Inc., 1965, all rights reserved.

## Man Is Separated

"For the wages of sin is death" (spiritual separation from God) (Romans 6:23).

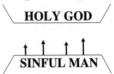

This diagram illustrates that God is holy and man is sinful. A great gulf separates the two. The arrows illustrate that man is continually trying to reach God and the abundant life through his own efforts, such as a good life, philosophy, or religion.

The third law explains the only way to bridge this gulf . . .

> **Law Three:** *Jesus Christ is God's only provision for man's sin. Through Him you can know and experience God's love and plan for your life.*

### He Died in Our Place

"But God demonstrates His own love toward us, in that while we were yet sinners, Christ died for us" (Romans 5:8).

### He Rose from the Dead

"Christ died for our sins . . . He was buried . . . He was raised on the third day according to the Scriptures . . . He appeared to [Peter], then to the twelve. After that He appeared to more than five hundred . . ." (1 Corinthians 15:3–6).

### He Is the Only Way to God

"Jesus said to him, 'I am the way, and the truth, and the life; no one comes to the Father, but through Me'" (John 14:6).

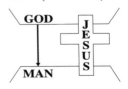

This diagram illustrates that God has bridged the gulf which separates us from Him by sending His Son, Jesus Christ, to die on the cross in our place to pay the penalty for our sins.

It is not enough just to know these three laws . . .

> ***Law Four:*** *We must individually receive Jesus Christ as Savior and Lord; then we can know and experience God's love and plan for our lives.*

## We Must Receive Christ

"But as many as received Him, to them He gave the right to become children of God, even to those who believe in His name" (John 1:12).

## We Receive Christ through Faith

"For by grace you have been saved through faith; and that not of yourselves, it is the gift of God; not as a result of works, that no one should boast" (Ephesians 2:8–9).

## When We Receive Christ, We Experience a New Birth

(Read John 3:1–8.)

## We Receive Christ by Personal Invitation

(Christ is speaking): "Behold, I stand at the door and knock; if any one hears My voice and opens the door, I will come in to him" (Revelation 3:20).

Receiving Christ involves turning to God from self (repentance) and trusting Christ to come into our lives to forgive our sins and to make us the kind of people He wants us to be. Just to agree intellectually that Jesus Christ is the Son of God and that He died on the cross for our sins is not enough. Nor is it enough to have an emotional experience. We receive Jesus Christ by faith, as an act of the will.

These two circles represent two kinds of lives:

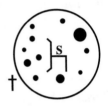

### SELF-DIRECTED LIFE

S— Self is on the throne
†— Christ is outside the life
●— Interests are directed by self, often resulting in discord and frustration

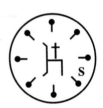

### CHRIST-DIRECTED LIFE

†— Christ is in the life and on the throne
S— Self is yielding to Christ
●— Interests are directed by Christ, resulting in harmony with God's plan

Which circle best represents your life?

Which circle would you like to have represent your life?

## You Can Receive Christ Right Now by Faith through Prayer

(Prayer is talking with God.)

God knows your heart and is not so concerned with your words as He is with the attitude of your heart. The following is a suggested prayer:

> *"Lord Jesus, I need You. Thank You for dying on the cross for my sins. I open the door of my life and receive You as my Savior and Lord. Thank You for forgiving my sins and giving me eternal life. Make me the kind of person You want me to be."*

Does this prayer express the desire of your heart?

If it does, pray this prayer right now, and Christ will come into your life, as He promised.

## APPENDIX B

*Have You Made the Wonderful Discovery*
*of the Spirit-Filled Life?* *

Everyday can be an exciting adventure for the Christian who knows the reality of being filled with the Holy Spirit and who lives constantly, moment by moment, under His gracious control.

The Bible tells us that there are three kinds of people:

1. NATURAL MAN (one who has not received Christ)

"But a natural man does not accept the things of the Spirit of God; for they are foolishness to him, and he cannot understand them, because they are spiritually appraised" (1 Corinthians 2:14).

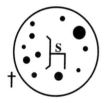

SELF-DIRECTED LIFE

S— Ego or finite self is on the throne
†— Christ is outside the life
●— Interests are controlled by self, often resulting in discord and frustration

2. SPIRITUAL MAN (one who is controlled and empowered by the Holy Spirit)

"But he who is spiritual appraises all things . . ." (1 Corinthians 2:15).

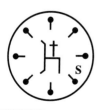

CHRIST-DIRECTED LIFE

†— Christ is on the throne of the life
S— Ego or self is dethroned
●— Interests are under control of infinite God, resulting in harmony with God's plan

3. CARNAL MAN (one who has received Christ, but who lives in defeat because he trusts in his own efforts to live the Christian life)

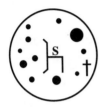

SELF-DIRECTED LIFE

S— Ego or finite self is on the throne
†— Christ is dethroned
●— Interests are controlled by self, often resulting in discord and frustration

"And I, brethren, could not speak to you as to spiritual men, but as to carnal men, as to babes in Christ. I gave you milk to drink, not solid food; for you were not yet able to receive it. Indeed, even now you are not yet able, for you are still carnal. For since there is jealousy and strife among you, are you not fleshly, and are you not walking like mere men?"(1 Corinthians 3:1–3).

**A. God has Provided for Us an Abundant and Fruitful Christian Life.**

Jesus said, "I came that they might have life, and might have it abundantly" (John 10:10).

"I am the vine, you are the branches; he who abides in Me, and I in him, he bears much fruit; for apart from Me you can do nothing" (John 15:5).

"But the fruit of the Spirit is love, joy, peace, patience, kindness, goodness, faithfulness, gentleness, self-control; against such things there is no law" (Galatians 5:22, 23).

"But you shall receive power when the Holy Spirit has come upon you; and you shall be My witnesses both in Jerusalem, and in all Judea and Samaria, and even to the remotest part of the earth" (Acts 1:8).

THE SPIRITUAL MAN

Some Personal Traits Which Result from Trusting God:

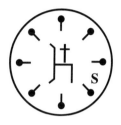

Christ-centered                                          Love
Empowered by the Holy Spirit                             Joy
Introduces others to Christ                              Peace
Effective prayer life                                    Patience
Understands God's Word                                   Kindness
Trusts God                                               Goodness
Obeys God                                                Faithfulness

The degree to which these traits are manifested in the life depends upon the extent to which the Christian trusts the Lord with every detail of his life, and upon his maturity in Christ. One who is only beginning to understand the ministry of the Holy Spirit should not be discouraged if he is not as fruitful as more mature Christians who have known and experienced this truth for a longer period.

*Why is it that most Christians are not experiencing the abundant life?*

**B. Carnal Christians Cannot Experience the Abundant and Fruitful Christian Life.**

The carnal man trusts in his own efforts to live the Christian life:

1. He is either uninformed about, or has forgotten, God's love, forgiveness, and power (Romans 5:8–10; Hebrews 10:1–25; 1 John 1; 2:1–3; 2 Peter 1:9; Acts 1:8).

2. He has an up-and-down spiritual experience.

3. He cannot understand himself—he wants to do what is right, but cannot.

4. He fails to draw upon the power of the Holy Spirit to live the Christian life.

(1 Corinthians 3:1–3; Romans 7:15–24; 8:7; Galatians 5:16–18)

## THE CARNAL MAN

Some or all of the following traits may characterize the Christian who does not fully trust God:

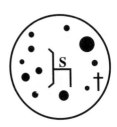

Ignorance of his
   spiritual heritage
Unbelief
Disobedience
Loss of love for God and
   for others
Poor prayer life
No desire for Bible study

Legalistic attitude
Discouragement
Impure thoughts
Jealousy
Guilt
Critical spirit
Worry
Frustration
Aimlessness

(The individual who professes to be a Christian but who continues to practice sin should realize that he may not be a Christian at all, according to 1 John 2:3; 3:6–9; Ephesians 5:5.)

*The third truth gives us the only solution to this problem . . .*

### C. Jesus Promised the Abundant and Fruitful Life as the Result of Being Filled (Controlled and Empowered) by the Holy Spirit.

The Spirit-filled life is the Christ-controlled life, by which Christ lives His life in and through us in the power of the Holy Spirit (John 15).

1. One becomes a Christian through the ministry of the Holy Spirit, according to John 3:1–8. From the moment of spiritual birth, the Christian is indwelt by the Holy Spirit at all times (John 1:12; Colossians 2:9–10; John 14:16–17). Though all Christians are indwelt by the Holy Spirit, not all Christians are filled (controlled and empowered) by the Holy Spirit.

2. The Holy Spirit is the source of the overflowing life (John 7:37–39).

3. The Holy Spirit came to glorify Christ (John 16:1–5). When one is filled with the Holy Spirit, he is a true disciple of Christ.

4. In His last command before His ascension, Christ promised the power of the Holy Spirit to enable us to be witnesses for Him (Acts 1:1–9).

*How, then, can one be filled with the Holy Spirit?*

**D. We Are Filled (Controlled and Empowered) by the Holy Spirit by Faith; Then We Can Experience the Abundant and Fruitful Life Which Christ Promised to Each Christian.**

You can appropriate the filling of the Holy Spirit *right now* if you:

1. Sincerely desire to be controlled and empowered by the Holy Spirit (Matthew 5:6; John 7:37–39).

2. Confess your sins.

   By faith thank God that He has forgiven all of your sins—past, present, and future—because Christ died for you (Colossians 2:13–15; 1 John 1; 2:1–3; Hebrews 10:1–17).

3. By faith claim the fullness of the Holy Spirit, according to:

   a. HIS COMMAND—Be filled with the Spirit. "And do not get drunk with wine, for that is dissipation, but be filled with the Spirit" (Ephesians 5:18).

   b. HIS PROMISE—He will always answer when we pray according to His will. "And this is the confidence which we have before Him, that, if we ask anything according to His will, He hears us. And if we know that He hears us in whatever we ask, we know that we have the requests which we have asked from Him" (1 John 5:14–15).

   *Faith can be expressed through prayer . . .*

**How to Pray in Faith to Be Filled with the Holy Spirit**

We are filled with the Holy Spirit by **faith** alone. However, true prayer is one way of expressing your faith. The following is a suggested prayer:

> *"Dear Father, I need You. I acknowledge that I have been in control of my life; and that, as a result, I have sinned against You. I thank You that You have forgiven my sins through Christ's death on*

121

> *the cross for me. I now invite Christ to again take control of the throne of my life. Fill me with the Holy Spirit as You commanded me to be filled, and as You promised in your Word that You would do if I asked in faith. I pray this in the name of Jesus. As an expression of my faith, I now thank You for taking control of my life and for filling me with the Holy Spirit."*

Does this prayer express the desire of your heart? If so, bow in prayer and trust God to fill you with the Holy Spirit right now.

## How to Know that You are Filled (Controlled and Empowered) by the Holy Spirit

Did you ask God to fill you with the Holy Spirit? Do you know that you are now filled with the Holy Spirit? On what authority? (On the trustworthiness of God Himself and His Word: Hebrews 11:6; Romans 14:22–23).

Do not depend upon feelings. The promise of God's Word, not our feelings, is our authority. The Christian lives by faith (trust) in the trustworthiness of God Himself and His Word. This train diagram illustrates the relationship between **fact** (God and His Word), **faith** (our trust in God and His Word), and **feeling** (the result of our faith and obedience) (John 14:21).

The train will run with or without the caboose. However, it would be futile to attempt to pull the train by the caboose. In the same way, we, as Christians, do not depend upon feelings or emotions, but we place our faith (trust) in the trustworthiness of God and the promises of His Word.

## How to Walk in the Spirit

Faith (trust in God and His promises) is the only means by which a Christian can live the Spirit-controlled life. As you continue to trust Christ moment by moment:

1. Your life will demonstrate more and more of the fruit of the Spirit (Galatians 5:22–23); and will be more and more conformed to the image of Christ (Romans 12:2; 2 Corinthians 3:18).

2. Your prayer life and study of God's Word will become more meaningful.

3. You will experience His power in witnessing (Acts 1:8).

4. You will be prepared for spiritual conflict against the world (1 John 2:15–17); against the flesh (Galatians 5:16–17); and against Satan (1 Peter 5:7–9; Ephesians 6:10–13).

5. You will experience His power to resist temptation and sin (1 Corinthians 10:13; Philippians 4:13; Ephesians 1:19–23; 6:10; 2 Timothy 1:7; Romans 6:1–16).

**Spiritual Breathing**

By faith you can continue to experience God's love and forgiveness.

If you become aware of an area of your life (an attitude or an action) that is displeasing to the Lord, even though you are walking with Him and sincerely desiring to serve Him, simply thank God that He has forgiven your sins—past, present and future—on the basis of Christ's death on the cross. Claim His love and forgiveness by faith and continue to have fellowship with Him.

If you retake the throne of your life through sin—a definite act of disobedience—breathe spiritually.

**Spiritual Breathing** (exhaling the impure and inhaling the pure) is an exercise in faith that enables you to continue to experience God's love and forgiveness.

1. **Exhale**—confess your sin—agree with God concerning your sin and thank Him for His forgiveness of it, according to 1 John 1:9 and Hebrews 10:1–25. Confession involves repentance—a change in attitude and action.

2. **Inhale**—surrender the control of your life to Christ, and appropriate (receive) the fullness of the Holy Spirit by faith. Trust that He now controls and empowers you, according to the *command* of Ephesians 5:18 and the *promise* of 1 John 5:14–15.

**About the Authors:**

Bob and Jan Horner have long been co-workers—as partners in marriage, parents of three daughters, staff members of Campus Crusade for Christ International, and speakers at Family Life Conferences.

Bob is a graduate of Westmont College and the University of Colorado in mechanical engineering. He joined the staff of Campus Crusade for Christ International in 1964. Jan became part of Campus Crusade two years later, after finishing her education at Colorado State University.

Together, Bob and Jan have invested over ten years in addressing the needs of couples. Their daughters are Kelley, Shawna, and Andrea—and they all love calling Boulder, Colorado, "home."